Secrets, Skeletons & Pedigrees

Secrets, Skeletons & Pedigrees

The Extraordinary Satterthwaite Sisters

BY

William M. Hartley

Also by the Author

The Hartleys: No Longer Shopkeepers – a Hartley Family progression
ISBN 978-1-904244-51-6

The Mellodews of Moorside: An Oldham Velvet Dynasty
ISBN 978-1-874181-64-4

Lancashire Cotton Spinners. A fortune made in the mills
ISBN 978-1-910837-06-1

Secrets, Skeletons & Pedigrees: The Extraordinary Satterthwaite Sisters

First published in 2019
by Palatine Books,
Carnegie House,
Chatsworth Road
Lancaster LA1 4SL
www.palatinebooks.com

Copyright © William M. Hartley

All rights reserved
Unauthorised duplication contravenes existing laws
The right of William M. Hartley to be identified as the author of this work has been asserted in accordance with the Copyright, Designs and Patents Act 1988
British Library Cataloguing-in-Publication data
A catalogue record for this book is available from the British Library
Paperback ISBN 13: 978-1-910837-25-2

Designed and typeset by Carnegie Book Production
www.carnegiebookproduction.com
Printed and bound in Great Britain by Severn

List of Contents

List of Illustrations	vii
Preface	x
Family Trees:	
The Hornby Family Tree	xii
The Sheridan/Gore Jones Family Tree	xiv
The Satterthwaite Family Tree	xvi
Chapters:	
1. Arrival in Buxton in reduced circumstances	1
– Solomon's Temple	7
2. The hunt for the Will – my introduction to the Satterthwaites	8
3. The aristocratic connection	14
4. Dalton Hall influence, the Living at Disley and yet more good connections	25
5. The Dark Secret	34
– A little aside – Sambo's Grave and Fanny's Hand	42
– Robert Gillow, the cabinet maker	45
6. In Chancery	47
7. The Sheridan Connection and Paternal Grandpapa	52
8. Life at Stonehurst – the first twenty years	60
9. Uncles, Aunts and Uncle Geoffie – a surprising disappointment	70
10. Continuing life at Stonehurst – the separate lives of Maud and Lettie	79
11. The Fire	85

12. Maud's Funeral	88
13. Lettie alone, the trip to Lichfield and an unseemly outrage	91
14. Matrons' Challenge	96
15. The Satterthwaite Bequest	99
Appendix showing map of Sunderland Point, Bazil, Glasson Dock and River Lune	104
Acknowledgements	105
Select Bibliography	107
Index	108

List of Illustrations

Chapter One

The Grange, Firs Road, Kenley (1916)	2
Maud, Letitia and Mary (1903)	3
Stamp of Tufnell Satterthwaite & Co. Ltd (1916)	4
Stonehurst, Green Lane, Buxton (1916)	5
Stonehurst – side view (2013)	5
Stonehurst through the trees in winter (2019)	5
Solomon's Temple, Grin Low, Buxton (2019)	7

Chapter Two

Evelyn Letitia and Beatrice Mary Satterthwaite (c.1916)	9
Maud Gertrude Satterthwaite as a young girl	9
Will of Beatrice Mary Satterthwaite	11

Chapter Three

Dressing set – a wedding gift from the 14th Earl of Derby	14
St Mary's Church, Disley, Cheshire	15
Canon Charles James Satterthwaite	16
Victoria Susan Satterthwaite (née Hornby)	16
Edward Geoffrey Smith Stanley, 14th Earl of Derby and three times Prime Minister	17
Miss Waller, the Hornbys' governess	18
Edward Smith Stanley, 13th Earl of Derby	19
Dalton Hall – the main front (pre-demolition)	20
Dalton Hall from across the park (pre-demolition)	21
Dalton Hall – the main staircase (pre-demolition)	22
Dalton Hall – landing – a watercolour by Victoria Susan Hornby	23
'Mother knitting at Dalton Hall' – a watercolour by Victoria Susan Hornby	23

viii SECRETS, SKELETONS & PEDIGREES

The new Dalton Hall (2014) –'the stately doll's house'	24
The new Dalton Hall (2014) showing the old entrance	24

CHAPTER FOUR

Disley Vicarage (1905)	26
'Charlie reading The Times at Disley Parsonage' (1879) – a watercolour by Victoria Susan Satterthwaite ('VSS')	27
Lyme Hall, (the South Front) Disley – the seat of the Legh family (Jarrold Publishing, 1990)	28
St. Oswald's Church, Winwick, Newton Le Willows (2018)	29
Admiral Sir Geoffrey Thomas Phipps Hornby (in retirement) at his seat of Lordington, Havant, Sussex	30
The Library at Lyme Hall – a watercolour by VSS	31
Charlie writing his sermon at Disley Parsonage (1879) – a watercolour by VSS	32

CHAPTER FIVE

Kinder from the garden, Disley Vicarage (1891) – a watercolour by VSS	35
St Helen's Church, Overton (2014)	36
Lancaster Castle (2019)	37
Sunderland Point (2017)	38
John Satterthwaite – a portrait by George Romney (*c.*1780)	40
The signpost to Sambo's Grave at Sunderland Point	43
Waring and Gillow Ltd, Oxford Street, London	45

CHAPTER SIX

A corner of the Quaker Burial Ground at Colthouse Town End, near Hawkshead (2019)	48
Petition to the House of Lords (an extract) (1821)	50

CHAPTER SEVEN

Bookplate to Johnson Dictionary (1755)	53
Launching of the tug *Maud* (1900)	57
The tug *Maud* (aquatint)	58

CHAPTER EIGHT

Charles Geoffrey Satterthwaite ('Uncle Geoffie')	61
Mrs Gertrude Mary Charlotte Satterthwaite, Lettie's mother (1933)	62
Francis Edmund Sheridan Satterthwaite ('Frank') at the onset of	

LIST OF ILLUSTRATIONS

First World War	64
Eton College Letter Heading (2017)	65
Broomcroft, Temple Road, Buxton, home of the Langford family (2019) now two dwellings	67
Lettie with two dogs outside Stonehurst (1927)	68

Chapter Nine

Broad Chalke Church ('All Saints'), near Salisbury (1899) (watercolour by VSS)	71
The Vicarage, Broad Chalke (1899) (watercolour by VSS)	71
Adelaide Wynne Pennant (later Mrs Edmund James Satterthwaite)	72
Restoration plaque at Broad Chalke Church	72
Uncle Geoffie as a boy at Disley Parsonage (a watercolour by VSS)	73
A Satterthwaite plate showing the raised sword dripping with drops of blood	73
Cross Hill, Torrisholme, near Morecambe	74
Uncle Geoffie at Cross Hill	75
Uncle Geoffie with his nurse (1934)	77
Newspaper headline (1935)	78

Chapter Ten

Mary with two dogs at Stonehurst	80
Lettie at Lytham with her dog	83

Chapter Eleven

Maud's room at Stonehurst – the left hand turret (2019)	86

Chapter Twelve

St Mary's Church, Dale Road, Buxton (2019)	89
The Satterthwaite grave at Christ Church, Burbage, Buxton	90

Chapter Thirteen

Lettie with dogs in her field	92
Newspaper picture showing the presentation of the Johnson Dictionary – *Lichfield Mercury* 9 July 1982	93

Chapter Fifteen

Bandstand in Pavilion Gardens, Buxton (2019)	101
War Memorial at St. Mary's Church, Buxton (2019)	102
The signature of Lettie on her Will (1984)	103

Preface

THIS LITTLE HISTOIRE WAS originally intended to describe the way of life of three unmarried characterful ladies living in a time warp in a large house in Buxton, Derbyshire, together with their widowed mother and bachelor brother.

It came about following a conversation at a party in Buxton where characters of the town were discussed. The Misses Satterthwaite were mentioned. As I had just finished my book about a Lancashire mill owning family, I was persuaded that I should put pen to paper.

I knew something of the family as I had acted in a professional capacity for the Misses Satterthwaite and had been told something of their history, not least that they considered themselves to be 'well connected'.

A little research revealed that they had aristocratic and landed gentry connections through the Earls of Derby of Knowsley Hall and the Hornby family of Dalton Hall, outside Lancaster.

The emergence of a series of diaries written in the age of Queen Victoria belonging to their grandmother and some wonderful watercolours painted by her meant that my story could not be confined to the ladies themselves. Their forebears were too important and interesting to be ignored.

Strong links to the historic City of Lancaster became apparent. Although a connection with trade had never been mentioned by the Buxton ladies, who regarded themselves as above commerce, it became clear that earlier Satterthwaites were heavily engaged in trade.

John Satterthwaite, who died in 1807, had married the daughter of a West Indian plantation owner and was a leading merchant in Lancaster. He is thought to have followed his father, Benjamin Satterthwaite, in importing mahogany for the well-known furniture maker Robert Gillow. He was an active trader between St. Kitts and Lancaster dealing in this and other commodities.

His father-in-law owned slaves and it is almost inevitable that John Satterthwaite had some influence in his father-in-law's business. Whilst a digression from the original intention of this book, this involvement was too fascinating to be left unmentioned particularly as it would appear to answer the conundrum as to the origin of the family's good fortune.

Other parts of their family were to prove to be no less interesting. The possession of a first edition of Dr Samuel Johnson's dictionary revealed the family's tie to the Sheridan family, of whom the playwright Richard Brinsley Sheridan is probably the best known.

As the history of the family unfolded, these Buxton ladies turned out to also have had connections with high ranking relatives in the Army, the Navy and the Church.

With this background and their Victorian values, it was not surprising that they kept themselves away from the popular throng. An exception was made in respect of dog shows. Two of the three sisters, one of whom had died before I was introduced to the household, were very knowledgeable about the canine world. That apart, they lived a life well removed from the ordinary and were a most singular household.

I hope that you will have as much fun reading about these characters and their family as I have had in researching their antecedents.

HORNBY FAMILY

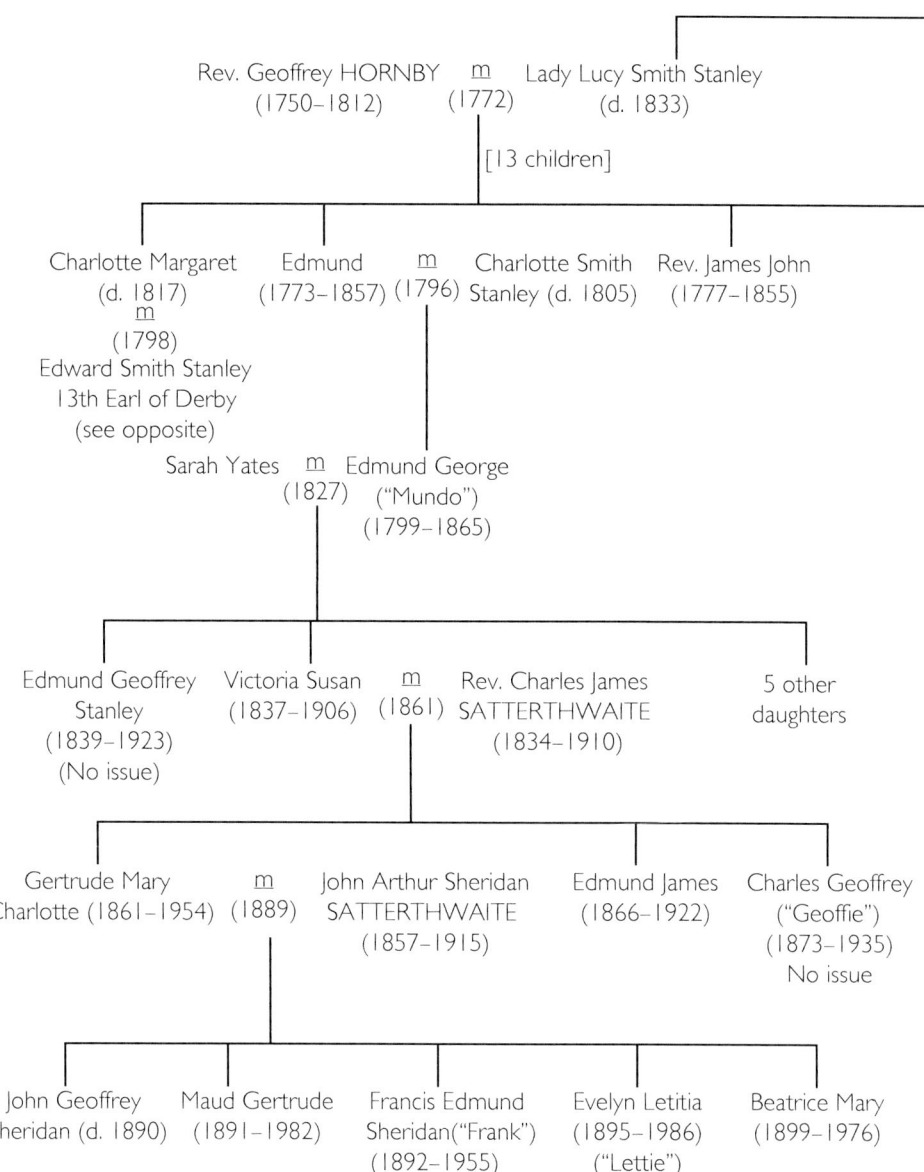

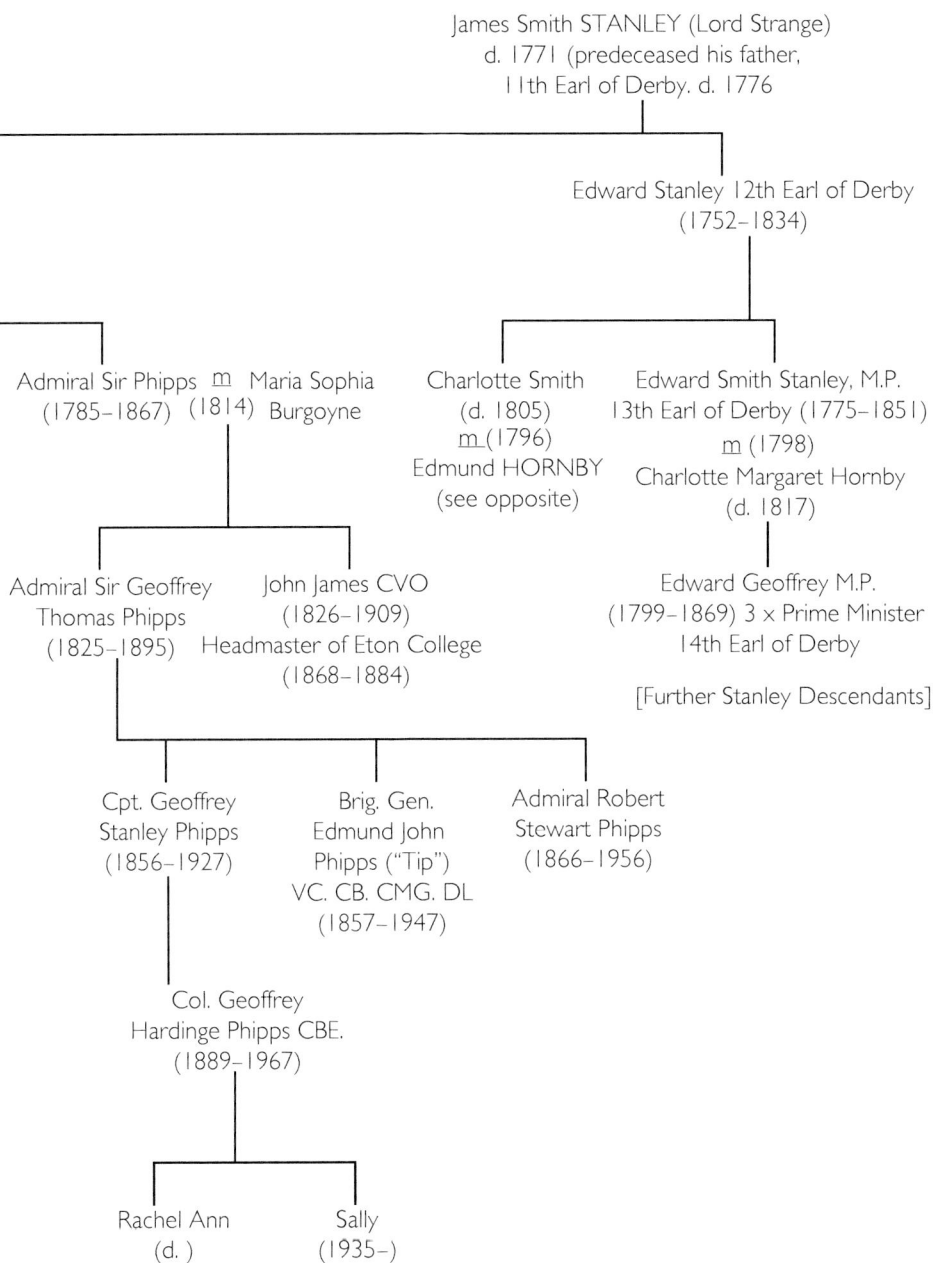

SHERIDAN / GORE-JONES FAMILIES

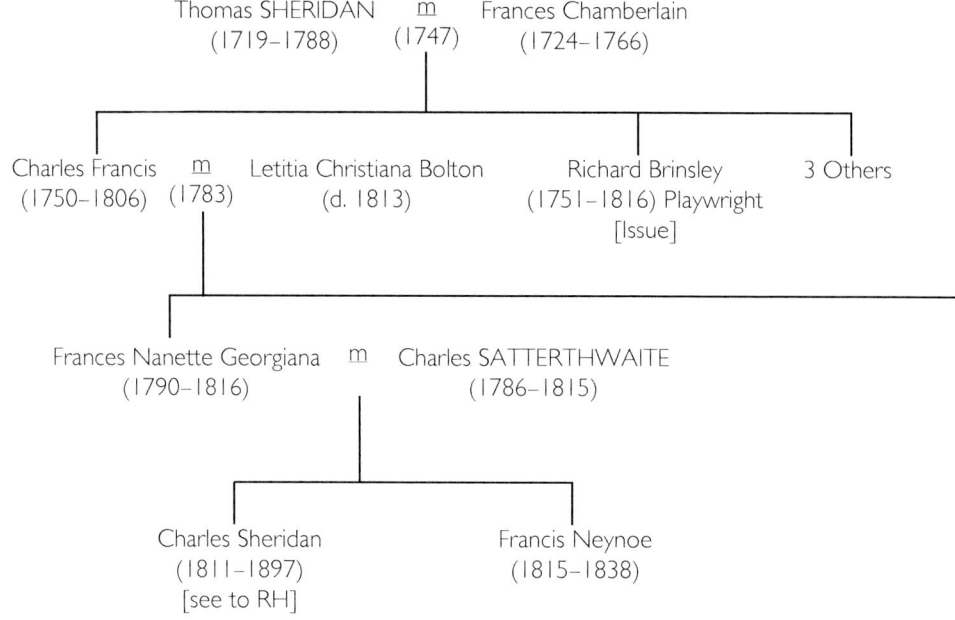

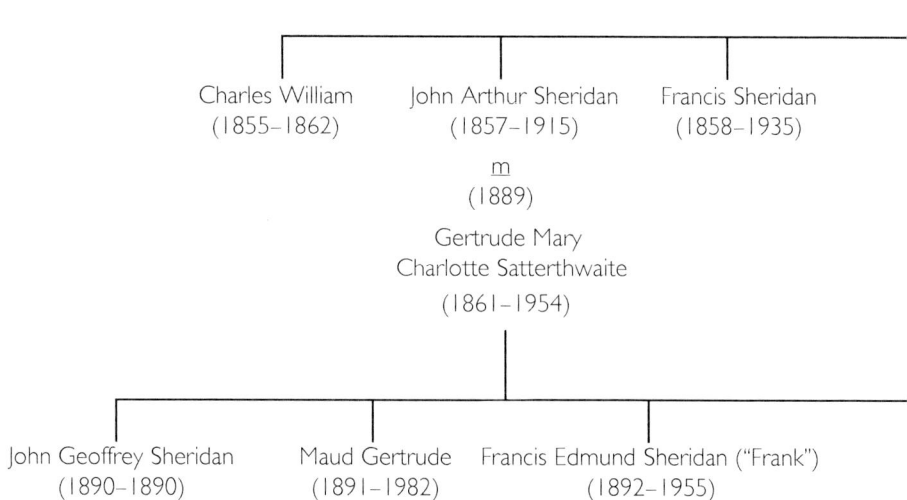

xv

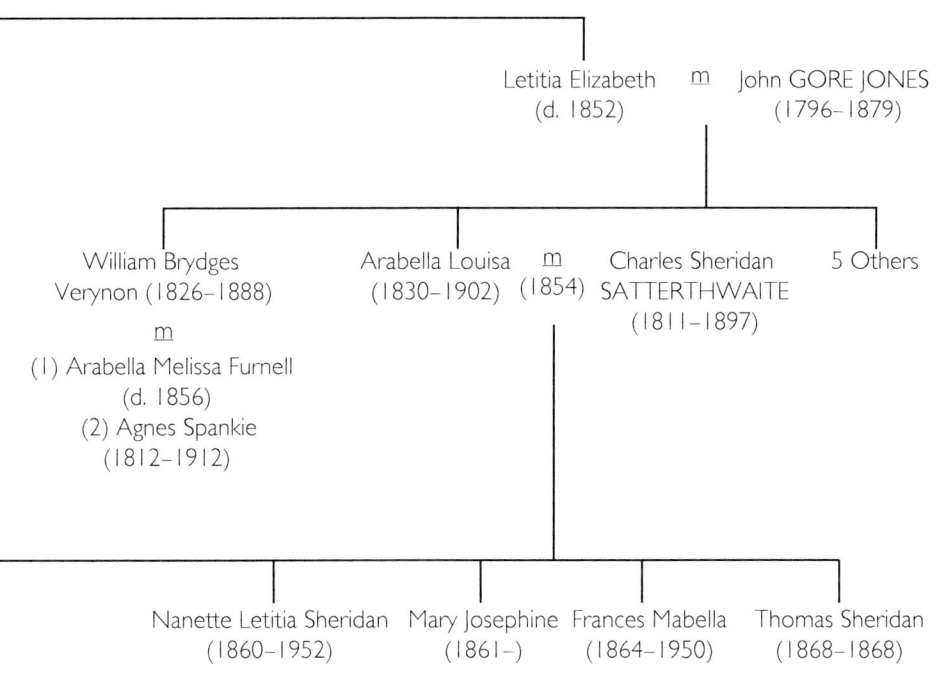

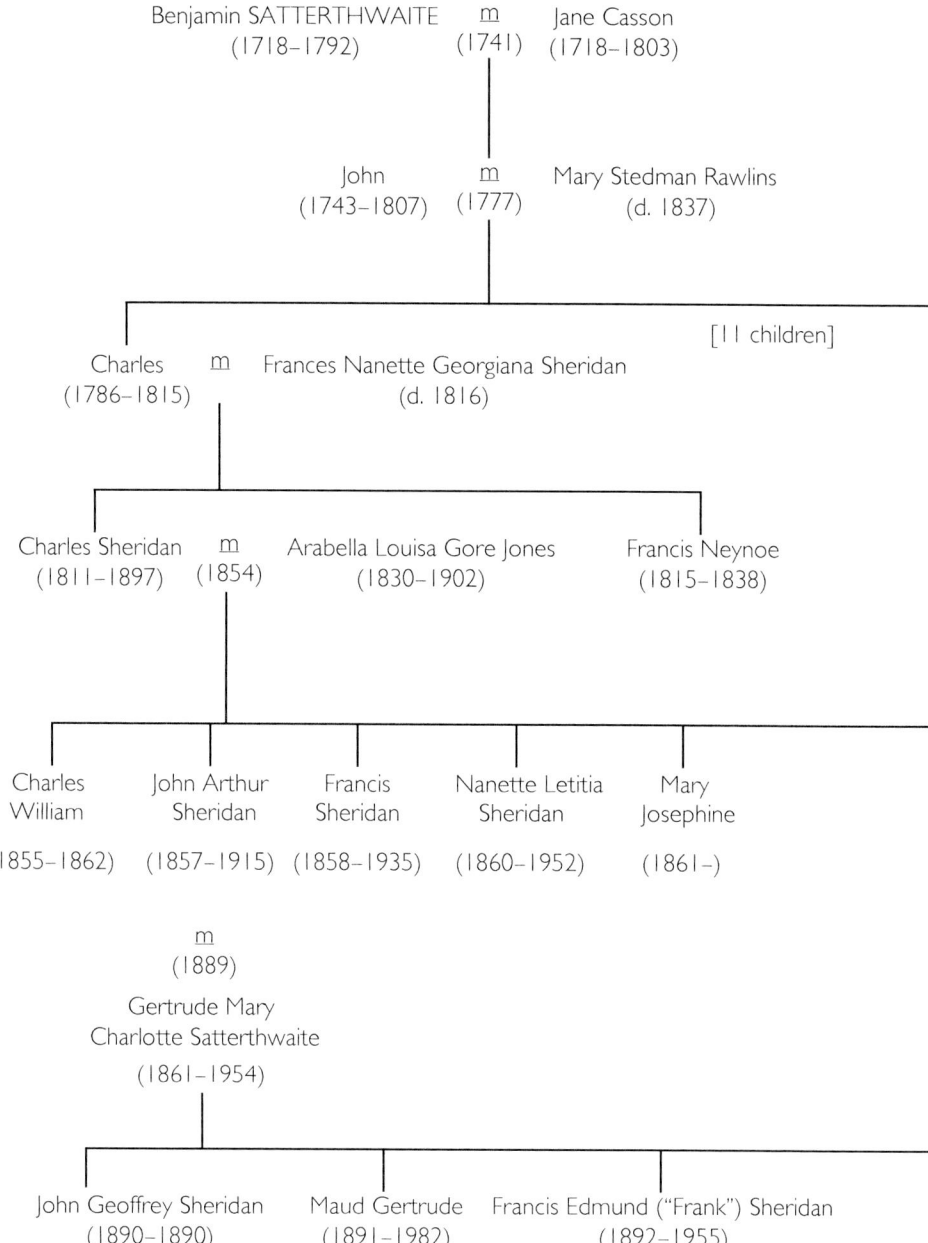

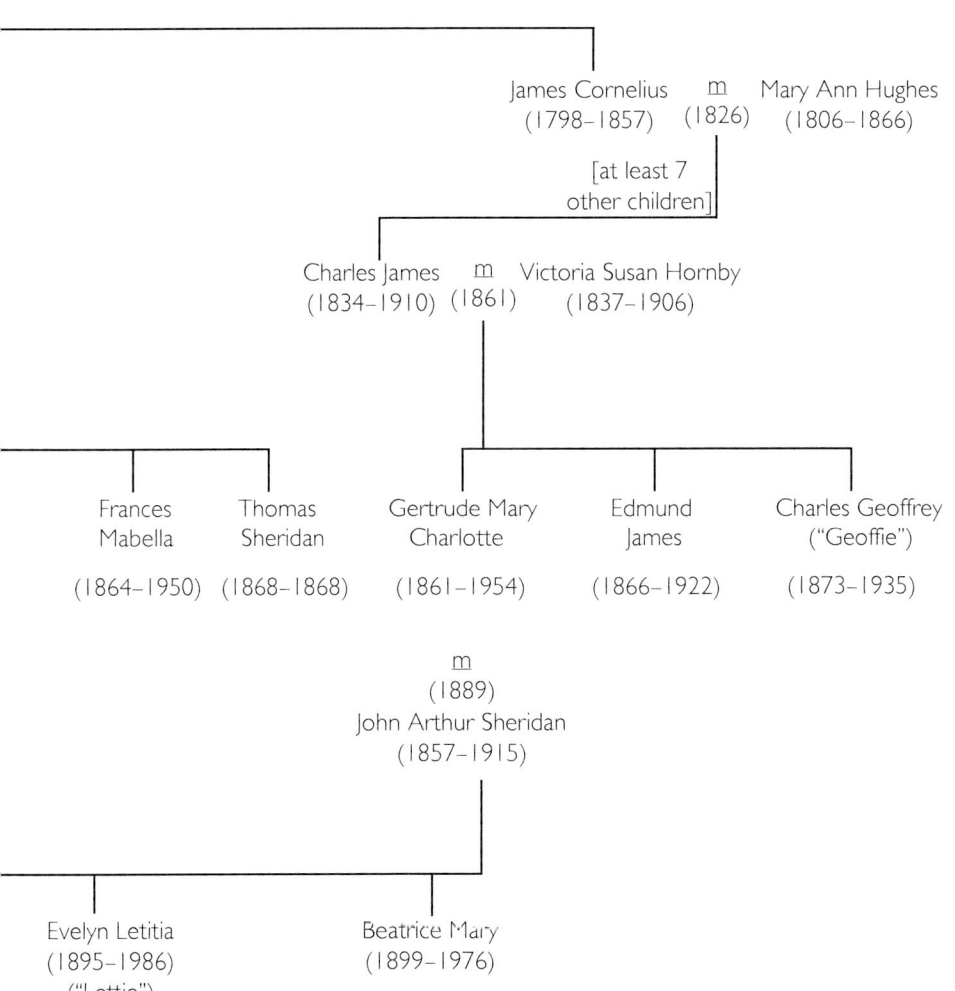

Chapter One

Arrival in Buxton in reduced circumstances

The recently widowed Mrs Satterthwaite and her three unmarried daughters arrived in Buxton, the Derbyshire Spa town, in 1916. Frank Satterthwaite, the son, was away at war and would not join the household until after the First World War had ended in November 1918.

It was made clear to the girls, Maud, then 25, Letitia, 21 and Mary, 17, that they would now be living in somewhat reduced circumstances compared with their previous way of life.

'Reduced circumstances' is of course a relative term, depending on the standards one had been used to.

The Grange at Firs Road, Kenley, south of Croydon, from which the family had removed, was a capacious dwelling. In addition to three reception rooms, a dining room measuring 22 feet by 15 feet, a drawing room 20 feet by 17 feet and a morning room 19 feet by 17 feet, there were eight bedrooms, a large billiard room (33 feet by 18 feet) and a conservatory. One bathroom seemed to be sufficient for the household.

The late Mr Satterthwaite and his wife and four children had enjoyed the service of three live-in staff, including a cook and a parlour maid. There were the usual kitchen quarters with a separate staircase to the maids' rooms.

The house had stood in extensive grounds. The Grange was approached by a long carriage drive; it had detached stabling and outbuildings, a gardener's cottage, two greenhouses, and coke and coal sheds. There was a kitchen garden, a tennis court, a croquet lawn and woodland. All in all this was a small estate amounting to some five and a half acres. Such grounds required full time outdoor staff.

John Sheridan Satterthwaite had died on 19 October 1915 aged 56. His death certificate gave his cause of death as 'Heart Disease. Heart block'.

The Grange, Firs Road, Kenley (1916)

That no inquest was ordered suggests that the deceased had been receiving medical attention prior to his death. He left an estate of £18,469 roughly equating to something in the order of £1,108,000 in today's money.

This included The Grange, which was sold after his death for nearly £5,500. That figure seems modest to us today for what was clearly a substantial property but house prices were very different then from what they are now.

Even in 1931 £700 would buy a four bedroomed detached house in a good area, which might be worth 1,000 times that figure now. Probably today The Grange would fetch something in the order of £5.5 million, which gives an indication of the sort of house it was.

Mrs Satterthwaite was left the income from her late husband's estate. He had been a Lloyds Underwriter and Insurance Broker, a principal in the firm of Tufnell Satterthwaite & Co Limited. He also had investments in railway, gas and electricity stocks, conventional investments for that time, together with shareholdings in the Thames Steam Tug and Lighterage Company Limited.

The widow also had money of her own. On the death of her father in 1910 the investments which had been placed in trust on her mother's marriage were divided between herself and her two brothers. It is not known how much these amounted to. Her father's own estate largely passed to her bachelor brother.

Although it would appear that Mrs Satterthwaite was comfortably placed financially, she was advised that without her husband's earned income she would have insufficient to allow her to maintain and staff a property the size of The Grange, even if she had wished to stay there.

There was the further fact that Britain was at war. In consequence, staff were hard to come by. Many men had joined the Armed Forces and many females had left domestic service to work in factories or on the farms. A move from The Grange, financial considerations apart, was not therefore entirely unexpected.

The move to Buxton was, in any event, logical. Mrs Satterthwaite had been brought up in nearby Disley and her younger brother, Charles Geoffrey Satterthwaite still lived there. Disley is 10 miles from Buxton and on the Buxton to Manchester railway line.

Furthermore, Buxton was considered to be respectable. It was still a Spa town, boasting several large hotels and hydrotherapy establishments. It had the magnificent eighteenth-century John Carr Crescent, an opera house and substantial pleasure gardens. It also had some decent sized houses. The town was surrounded by the rugged countryside of the High Peak.

So, although economies would have to be made, largely in respect of staff, Buxton had considerable attractions. There was also the expectation that it would prove to have a cheaper way of life than London's south east.

Maud, Letitia and Mary (1903)

Stamp of Tufnell Satterthwaite & Co. Ltd (1916)

At first Mrs Satterthwaite took a lease on the house in Green Lane, Buxton, known as Stonehurst. She subsequently bought the freehold from Mr Morton in 1918 and the two fields opposite respectively in 1924 and 1928, both from the Chatsworth estate.

Green Lane, then as now, was a good area. In 1916 it boasted a number of capacious houses of similar size to Stonehurst, with good proportioned houses on adjacent College and Temple Roads. Buxton College, which opened on its Green Lane site in 1881 after two centuries elsewhere in the town, was nearby. Surrounded by its playing fields it added to the rural feel of the area.

Stonehurst stood well. It was a large stone-built Victorian detached house. It had three storeys and cellars. Whilst it had garden on all four sides, however, it could not be described as standing in extensive grounds.

The views from the first and second floor windows commanded a vista across open fields to the Grin Low Woods and Solomon's Temple, which rough stone tower still stands as a landmark above the town today. In short, this was a house of substance, standing in a good area within walking distance of the town centre and with open countryside on its doorstep.

The interior of the house was commodious enough. The wide front door and tiled entrance porch led into the hall which stretched the depth of the house. Brown linoleum covered the floor. At the end of this hall stood a green baize door. Little seen now, such a door was usual in a big house. The idea was that the baize deadened any sound and smells from the kitchen beyond and that the door marked the entrance to the domestic region of the house.

Through this green baize door access was gained to the large kitchen, with its clothes drying rack hanging from the ceiling above the fireplace, a back scullery and the pantries. The fire consisted of a range with the open fire in the centre and ovens on either side. This range provided the hot water required for the kitchen and bathroom. There was no central heating.

Stonehurst, Green Lane, Buxton, in 1916, a side view in 2013 and through the trees in winter, 2019

A secondary staircase, the back stairs as they were called, ran from the kitchen to the top of the house. The domestic staff could thus go about their duties without meeting the principal occupants of the house on the main staircase.

From the kitchen there was also a stone stairway leading to the extensive cellars below. Coal and coke was kept down here delivered through an outside trapdoor.

In addition to the hall and kitchen area, the ground floor also comprised a large dining room, some 30 feet in length, a substantial drawing room facing on to the front garden, with a big bay window, a more modest but good sized front sitting room and a cloakroom with wc.

From the hall a wide handsome wooden staircase led to the upper floors.

The first floor contained four bedrooms, and the one bathroom and a separate wc. One bathroom was deemed sufficient for the household at a time when many lesser dwellings had no bathroom at all. Each bedroom was equipped with a washstand and towel rack and water could be brought up to those rooms via the back stairs.

The top floor comprised a further three bedrooms and various storerooms, including what became a photographic darkroom and amateur radio room.

Outbuildings consisted of a wash-house, wc and gardener's store together with a small animal pen. There was no garage.

It was felt that the employment of one man for one day per week would suffice to keep the garden in check. Domestic staff would consist of staff who could come in daily to cook and clean. This was a considerable reduction from the number of staff required to run The Grange. There was no suggestion that Mrs Satterthwaite nor her daughters would engage in any domestic work.

This then was a suitable house. It stood in a good position. It was sufficiently large to accommodate Mrs Satterthwaite and her four children. It could be run without live-in domestic staff. And, it had the added bonus of being lit by electricity. Each room had a single drop light.

And so it was to this house that Mrs Satterthwaite and her daughters removed, all of them to remain there until their respective deaths, with the house being sold some 70 years later in 1986 following Lettie's demise. The house still stands although now converted into two decent sized dwellings.

Of course, it might have been expected that all three daughters might marry. They did not do so. Firstly, the First World War reduced the number of eligible men available, and secondly it has been said that Mrs Satterthwaite discouraged the idea. She warned her girls that the only suitable men they might probably meet would be from within the extensive Satterthwaite family. As we shall see, there were several instances where cousins had married cousins. It is thought that she counselled her daughters that if they did the same any offspring might not be 'quite right'.

As a Miss Satterthwaite, she herself had married a Satterthwaite, albeit a first cousin once removed.

A more likely explanation for her reluctance to encourage her daughters to marry is that she wanted to keep the girls at home for companionship in her old age. If that was so, she achieved her aim!

Solomon's Temple, Grin Low, Buxton

Solomon's Temple, also known as Grin Tower, is a Victorian tower standing about 1440 feet above sea level, three quarters of a mile from the centre of Buxton. It is about half a mile from Stonehurst and would be reached by walking up through Grin Low Woods.

These woods now form a Country Park and are maintained by the Buxton Civic Association. Adjacent is Poole's Cavern, also open to the public.

The tower was built by Solomon Mycock in 1896 to provide work for some of the locally unemployed. It was paid for by public subscription with assistance from the 7th Duke of Devonshire.

The structure is a 20 feet high two storey tower built on top of a bronze-age barrow. It contains nothing other than a staircase to the top floor from which there are good views over the town and surrounding countryside of the Peak District.

It was restored in 1998; the Satterthwaite Bequest (see Chapter 15) contributed towards its restoration.

Solomon's Temple, Grin Low, Buxton (2019)

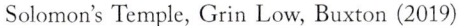

CHAPTER TWO

The hunt for the Will – my introduction to the Satterthwaites

In August 1976 I received a telephone call from the manager of National Westminster Bank in Buxton asking if I would attend upon a Miss Satterthwaite of Green Lane, whose sister had recently died.

I had been brought up in Buxton and I recalled the Misses Satterthwaite. There always seemed to be two of them walking in the vicinity of Green Lane and Grin Low Woods, accompanied by one or two dogs. They always struck me as tall and imposing and they were certainly distinctive with their long brown coats and brown flat brimmed felt hats. The impression given was that they were of another age.

I pulled the bell at Stonehurst, and waited. This gave me time to take in the impressive size of the house and to realize that its occupants, however many there might be, were probably old.

The hedges standing higher than the limestone walls which surrounded the garden were well tended and the flower beds were maintained. But I could see through the windows that the linings to the curtains were in shreds and certainly the house needed a good lick of paint. There was no evidence of a motor car, driveway or garage.

Eventually, the wide front door was opened by a tall elderly lady, accompanied by a large black dog. She introduced herself as Miss Letitia Satterthwaite. I was invited into her sitting room to the right of the front door.

As I followed her, I was able to take in the long hall, its floor covered by linoleum and its walls well covered in pictures. At the far end I could see a door covered in green baize. A wide wooden staircase obviously led to the upper floors.

Although it was August, there was a coal fire burning in the old fashioned grate on the left hand side of the hall.

Evelyn Letitia and Beatrice Mary Satterthwaite (left, c.1916), and
Maud Gertrude Satterthwaite (right) as a young girl

The room that I entered was furnished in the Victorian manner, a tall dresser on one side, a large oak bureau on another, a number of upholstered chairs of an upright nature, an armchair on either side of the fireplace, odd tables dotted around the room covered with piles of magazines and newspapers, and the floor carpeted, albeit threadbare, with the odd rug here and there.

There were many pictures on the walls, the most striking of which was a painting of a Thames Tug boat called "Lettie".

I judged that the room, with its tall brown skirting boards and faded wallpaper, had not been decorated for many, many years. However, in spite of a feeling of neglect, there was a coal fire blazing in the black leaded grate, which took the chill off this lofty room.

I was invited to take a seat, a space being cleared on a chair for that purpose. The dog took its place in front of the fire. Miss Satterthwaite took a seat to the left of the fireplace from which she could observe anyone who approached the house through the front garden gate.

Miss Satterthwaite explained that her younger sister, Beatrice Mary (always called 'Mary'), had died aged 77 and that she understood I could deal with her late sister's estate. I had apparently been recommended as a solicitor by her doctor, Dr Langwell, and by the manager at National Westminster Bank.

I asked if there was a Will. The answer was in the affirmative; Miss Satterthwaite and her late sister had apparently both signed wills on a W. H. Smith Will Form in 1952, prior to travelling to a dog show in Lytham St. Annes. They had left their respective estates to each other.

I asked if I could see the Will. There was a long silence. Miss Satterthwaite had apparently looked for the Will but could not find it. However, she was clear that her late sister intended that she should inherit her estate. She asked what the position would be if the Will could not be found.

I realised that I knew nothing of this family. I did not know who lived in this large house. I was faced with an alert and intelligent old lady living in a commodious old-fashioned house, with a dog, but I knew not who else. Dressed in a long brown skirt, woollen stockings and several brown cardigans, with no make-up or jewellery, white hair escaping from its bun, with a clear upper class voice, this lady was unusual and definitely different from most of my clients.

Her manner of her speech was quite distinctive. She had the old fashioned characteristic of dropping her 'g's' when speaking. Thus, she went 'walkin'; she was 'readin' and 'listenin' when I arrived.

I was going to have to ask some questions, but with care. There could be siblings or nephews and nieces of a deceased brother or sister.

At this moment, I was told not to speak further. The Coal Boy had apparently arrived and discourse could not proceed until he had brought in coals and stoked the fire.

I expected a spotty boy of 12 or more and was a little surprised when a man of 70 appeared, coal buckets in hand. He was apparently to stoke the fires in this sitting room, the hall and the kitchen. I was told that coal was brought up from the cellars below and the fires were stoked twice a day.

The Coal Boy's departure allowed me to ascertain that Miss Satterthwaite's parents and unmarried brother were dead but that she had an elder unmarried sister, Maud, who lived elsewhere in the house. Discreetly I enquired if any of her siblings had had children. If they had, even if illegitimate, such children in the absence of a will might have an interest in Mary's estate. Her answer was in the negative but it was clear that no offence had been taken at the question.

On this basis, I explained that unless the will of her late sister Mary could be found her estate would devolve as on intestacy between Maud

This is the last Will and Testament

of me Beatrice Mary Satterthwaite of "Stonehurst" Green Lane Buxton in the County of Derbyshire made this Twenty first day of July in the year of our Lord one thousand nine hundred and fifty two

I HEREBY revoke all Wills made by me at any time heretofore. I appoint my sister Evelyn Letitia Satterthwaite of "Stonehurst" Buxton Derbyshire to be my Executor, and direct that all my Debts and Funeral Expenses shall be paid as soon as conveniently may be after my decease.

I GIVE AND BEQUEATH unto my said sister Evelyn Letitia Satterthwaite all my estate and effects, real and personal which I may die possessed of, or entitled to

B. M. Satterthwaite

Signed by the said TESTATOR in the presence of us, present at the same time, who at her request, in her presence, and in the presence of each other, have subscribed our names as witnesses.

B. M. Satterthwaite

R. J. Andrew
Westminster Bank Ltd.,
Buxton — Bank Clerk

[signature]
Westminster Bank Ltd
Bank Manager Buxton

Will of Beatrice Mary Satterthwaite

and Letitia equally. I was told very firmly that this was not desirable and, again, not what her late sister had intended. It was clear that they had been close, sharing a common interest in dogs. The nuance was that Maud was probably "not all there".

It was thought that Mary might have had her Will in her room and I suggested that we had better look for it there. This was quite exciting as it meant that I would see a little more of this intriguing house.

I followed Lettie, as we shall now call her, along the hall wondering as I did so who cleaned the 40 feet of linoleum that stretched its length. We climbed the wide wooden staircase to the first floor. The dark wood stained door to Mary's room was unlocked by Lettie.

At first I thought we had entered a furniture store. The room was full of chests of drawers, cabinets, a davenport, other writing tables, suitcases, chairs, a washstand, wardrobe, towel rack, books and papers. Prints and pictures hung on the walls in no particular sort of order. The curtains were thin and unlined. There appeared to be no article of comfort. In one corner stood an old-fashioned narrow iron bedstead. This was Mary's room. Tidiness had obviously not been of major concern for its late occupant.

I knew we were to look for the Will, but where to start, and how much money, if any, did this household have? It was a big house, there was a coal boy, the garden was kempt, but no money that I could see had been spent on its interior or on its inhabitant's clothing for very many years. Were they very rich and parsimonious or utterly impoverished and struggling to make ends meet?

The first drawer opened yielded a Bank of England stock certificate. Further drawers contained other certificates, dividend vouchers (some uncashed) and bank statements. Mary, thankfully, had not been entirely without assets.

An hour of searching produced a quantity of stock and share certificates, premium savings bonds and evidence of bank accounts, but no Will!

Lettie again asked for confirmation that in the absence of a Will, her sister's money was to be divided between herself and her sister Maud. I so confirmed. She replied that she knew there was a Will and she would find it. It was time for me to go and leave Lettie to her search.

As I descended the staircase I came across a slight, short, elderly lady hovering at the bottom of the stairs. She wore glasses and was stooped. Lettie said 'this is Maud', and passed on. There was no formal introduction. I bid Maud 'good morning', followed Lettie and was shown to the front door. Lettie was adamant that she would find the Will.

Back at my office, I mused as to how the household at Stonehurst managed. Who cooked? Who cleaned? What did the two elderly ladies, Maud aged 85 and Lettie aged 81 do all day? Did they have enough money to keep this large old-fashioned house with its coal fires going?

A telephone call to my office at 9 o'clock next morning from Lettie confirmed that she had found the Will. I enquired of her where it had been found; that apparently was not material! It put me in mind of one of my partners who found the Will he was looking for in the corsets of his deceased client – along, in that case, with several stock certificates. I never did ascertain where Mary's Will had been found.

Lettie had said that her sister's Will had been written on a W. H. Smith Will Form. A solicitor is often apprehensive about a 'home made will' as it is not uncommon for changes to have been made after signing which gives rise to difficulties. However, I need not have worried. The Will was quite in order. Everything was left to Lettie, who was appointed as sole executrix. The Will was properly signed and witnessed by two bank officials. There had been no changes so all was well.

In the event, Mary's estate, including her one third share of the house, was agreed with the Inland Revenue at just over £47,000.

Shares in Transport Development Group and Sun Life of Canada almost exactly mirrored in number those held by Lettie as did the holdings of Government securities, War Loan, Treasury Stock and the like. The inheritance, assuming that Lettie had similar assets, would not make her a rich woman but it did provide her with some reassurance that she could cover the costs of running Stonehurst. It certainly reassured me that with some financial contribution from Maud, the modest Satterthwaite way of life could continue.

The partial foundation of their way of life is covered in my next chapter.

Chapter Three

The aristocratic connection

Over the years that I knew her, Lettie mentioned from time to time, with a certain hauteur, that she was well connected. There were references to the Earl of Derby and to Dalton Hall.

These references were backed up by a most impressive lady's dressing table case that I was shown. With all its bottles and brushes, this case was said to have been a gift to Lettie's maternal grandmother from the Earl of Derby at the time of her marriage.

I was also shown a book of lovely watercolours painted by her grandmother which included pictures of Dalton Hall and of Disley Vicarage.

Then there was what I was told was the Satterthwaite Crest – a raised sword dripping with drops of blood.

How these connections were intertwined was never explained and so when I set out to write a book about the Satterthwaites I thought I had better find out. The whereabouts of Dalton Hall had never been mentioned other than it was near Lancaster.

A copy of Lettie's parents' marriage certificate provided the first step in my enquiry.

This showed that her late father John Arthur Sheridan Satterthwaite (the 'Arthur' was dropped by the time he made his Will in 1914) then aged 32 had married her mother, Gertrude Mary Charlotte Satterthwaite, then

Dressing set – a wedding gift from the 14th Earl of Derby

St Mary's Church, Disley, July 2013

aged 27, on 5 March 1889 at St. Mary's Church, Disley, Cheshire. The certificate confirmed that Gertrude's father, the Reverend Charles James Satterthwaite, was vicar of the parish at that time. This then was Lettie's maternal grandfather.

The puzzle as to how a Satterthwaite married someone also called Satterthwaite will be dealt with later.

Details of this marriage seemed to bring me no nearer to the aristocratic connection. A perusal of 'Who was Who 1897–1916' however provided the vital information needed:

'Rev. Charles James Satterthwaite, Vicar of Disley, and an honorary canon of Chester Cathedral, was the son of James Cornelius Satterthwaite, late of Lancaster, and had married Victoria Susan Hornby, daughter of E. G. Hornby of Dalton Hall, Burton in Westmoreland, in 1861'. Victoria Susan Hornby was therefore Lettie's maternal grandmother.

So there one had the connection to Dalton Hall, which is some 10 miles north east of Lancaster.

A look at the website for Dalton Hall provided the further link needed: 'the Hornby family, originally from the Lancashire Fylde, had lived and

Canon Charles James Satterthwaite;
Victoria Susan Satterthwaite
(née Hornby)

held the Manor of Dalton since the late 1700s with a boost to their finances enjoyed by an advantageous marriage in 1796 by Edmund Hornby to his cousin Lady Charlotte [Smith] Stanley, daughter of the 12th Earl of Derby'.

To put the financial advantage in perspective, it is said that Edmund Hornby received a 4 per cent annuity charged on his wife's marriage settlement of £28,000 (roughly equivalent to £1.5 million today). This 4% would amount to £1,120 per annum (roughly £63,000 today), a useful sum and an amount which would allow for a very comfortable existence at that time, particularly if Edmund Hornby also had some money of his own.

This Edmund Hornby (1773–1857) was Victoria Susan's grandfather, so there one had the aristocratic connection by reason of his marriage.

The cousinly relationship mentioned was the result of the marriage between his father the Reverend Geoffrey Hornby (1750–1812) and Lady Lucy Stanley in 1772. She was the sister of Edward Stanley who later became the 12th Earl of Derby in 1776.

The Stanleys and the Hornbys were further linked by the marriage in 1798 between Edmund Hornby's sister, Charlotte Margaret Hornby, to Edward Smith Stanley, who became the 13th Earl of Derby in 1834.

This meant of course that Victoria Susan was the great niece of the 13th Earl of Derby and whilst this might seem a somewhat distant relationship, it was no doubt significant, particularly when one's father's cousin, the 14th Earl, became prime minister.

Today the Stanley family might be best remembered for the foundation of the 'Derby' horse race and the Knowsley Safari Park. In the nineteenth century the Stanleys had a higher profile than today; they were very important. They were also very rich. The 13th Earl (1775–1851) paid for the erection of a large number of schools and churches, largely within the neighbourhood of their seat at Knowsley Hall, near Prescot, between Liverpool and Warrington.

The Stanleys were also very influential. The 14th Earl (1799–1869) held the office of Prime Minister in 1852, 1858–9 and 1866–8.

Edward Geoffrey Smith Stanley, 14th Earl of Derby and three times Prime Minister

Miss Waller, the Hornbys' governess

Whilst it is not my intention to concentrate on the politics of nineteenth-century England, it is perhaps useful to remind the reader how important the Stanleys were to some of the events of that time, which would not go un-noticed by their relatives and other well-connected families.

Prior to becoming Prime Minister in 1852, soon after the death of his father, Edward Geoffrey Smith Stanley (14th Earl of Derby 1799–1869) had been Under Secretary for the Colonies 1827–8, Secretary for Ireland 1830–3 and Secretary for War and the Colonies 1833–4 and 1841–5.

The vicissitudes of nineteenth-century politics are somewhat forgotten today. His first administration only lasted from February to December 1852 whilst his second ministry lasted from February 1858 to March 1859.

He might have been described as 'hopeless' by some, being 'devoted to whist, billiards, racing and betting', but he was still powerful. In 1861 he organised relief in Lancashire to ameliorate the distress caused by the Cotton Famine when there was a cessation of cotton supplies to Lancashire by reason of the American Civil War. This lack of supplies effectively brought the Lancashire cotton spinning industry to a halt, putting huge numbers of people out of work.

It was the 14th Earl's last administration that was probably his most effective. His term of office saw the passing of the Reform Act 1867, steered through the House of Commons by Benjamin Disraeli. The Act greatly increased the number of people who had the vote; it added 938,000 voters to an electorate of 1,056,000 in England and Wales. Subsequent Stanleys continued to engage in politics but by then the connection with the Hornbys had somewhat lessened.

Edmund Hornby, having married a Stanley, also engaged in politics. One suspects that his political engagement was not out of inclination but more to appease his powerful father-in-law, who had disapproved of his marriage to his daughter. He was returned as MP for Preston in 1812. As a practising barrister on the Northern Circuit he could cope with the oratory required of an MP. However, apart from declaring that he was against universal suffrage and the secret ballot, he seems to have made little mark.

He remained an MP until 1826 when one of the Stanleys took over the seat, also as a Whig politician.

In general, it would appear that the Hornbys preferred to limit their influence to the locality of Lancaster.

A look at the 1841 Census showed Edmund George Hornby, the MP's son, (always known as 'Mundo') living at Castle Park, Lancaster (adjacent to Lancaster Castle) together with his wife Sarah, and six children including Victoria Susan. His father, brother-in-law to the 14th Earl of Derby, was living at Dalton Hall.

In addition to the family, the Census shows the house at Castle Park housing a governess and 11 other servants living at the property. This is an impressive household and certainly befitted a man who described himself as being of 'independent means' and who was Constable of Lancaster Castle and High Sheriff of Lancaster in 1828.

It is in the later Census return of 1851 which confirms, if such is needed, the connection between the Hornbys and the Stanleys.

On Sunday 30 March 1851, the date of the Census, Victoria Susan with her siblings, Miss Waller, the governess, and five servants are shown as being at 42 Castle Park, Lancaster. The Hornby parents were absent.

The father, Mundo, and his wife Sarah, are listed as being at Knowsley Hall. Mundo is described in the Census as 'nephew of the Earl'. He is shown to be a magistrate and Deputy Lord Lieutenant of Lancashire.

The Hornbys were guests of Edward Smith Stanley, 13th Earl of Derby, who was then a widower aged 75 and was to die later that year. His wife, Mundo's aunt, had died much earlier in 1817.

Edward Smith Stanley,
13th Earl of Derby

Dalton Hall – the main front, pre-demolition

As an aside, the 1851 Census is revealing in showing the extent of the Earl of Derby's household on the night of the Census. In addition to the family and guests, Knowsley Hall also housed four coachmen, three postilions, a butler, an under butler, three footmen, two valets, a cook and other servants numbering 32 in all. There was also a domestic chaplain.

Of course, some guests might have brought their own servants with them, but nevertheless the census shows a substantial household, all of whom would expect to be fed! Details of the outdoor staff are not given.

Following his father's death in November 1857 Mundo decided that he and his family should leave Lancaster and live at Dalton Hall. It first had to be modernised and extended. The family did not move in until 1860. The watercolours by Victoria Susan give an idea of the extent of the house.

The hall stood well with sloping gardens into the hillside on one side and an impressive approach up a curving drive from the Lancaster road below, ending in a sweep before the front door. The house itself boasted nine large windows on its garden front, which was often used as a background to visitor and family photographs.

The front door opened onto a substantial entrance porch, a porte-cochère as it is called, which allowed visitors to alight from a carriage whilst being sheltered from the elements.

Dalton Hall – from across the park – pre-demolition

The entrance hall was imposing, the staircase sweeping down from two sides before joining the single flight which descended to a tiled hallway. There is no record of the other rooms in the house but its extent can be gauged from the watercolour painted by Victoria Susan whose artistic use of the mirror conveys an even larger landing corridor than was obviously the case.

There is no evidence that Victoria Susan visited her Stanley relatives at Knowsley Hall or that she had any contact with her Stanley cousins. It is clear however from a number of family photographs that, following her marriage to Rev. Satterthwaite, she was a regular visitor to Dalton Hall.

When her father ('Mundo') died in 1865, aged 66, her brother Edmund Geoffrey Stanley Hornby took on the estate and remained at Dalton until his own death in 1923. He had no children.

Although there are photographs showing Lettie's mother, Gertrude, as a little girl visiting Dalton Hall, there is no record that she did so once she was married. In any event her early married life was spent in the south of England. Nor is there any record or hearsay evidence that Lettie and her brother and sisters visited Dalton. Possibly by then the connection had become a little tenuous – after all, how many people visit their great uncle? In any event, travel between Kenley, or later from Buxton, would not have been easy.

Dalton Hall – the main staircase – pre-demolition

One suspects that by the time of Mrs Satterthwaite's death in 1954 all contact with Dalton Hall had been lost.

However, the recital of life at Dalton from Lettie's mother and her uncle and the importance of the Stanleys must have rubbed off on the Satterthwaite girls. Such recitals would have reminded them that they were indeed well connected. As we shall see, Lettie could also boast of other important connections.

By 1966, at the time of the death of Charles Windham Leycester Penrhyn-Hornby, to whom possession of the hall had passed, Dalton Hall had fallen into disrepair and was riddled with rot of many sorts. It would also have been a rather large house to maintain. Mr Anthony Fielden Mason-Hornby, who inherited the Hall, was advised by his friend Sir Bertram Clough Williams-Ellis, the creator of Port Merion in North Wales, to 'pull it down'. So he did!

Dalton Hall
- the landing
(watercolour by
Victoria Susan
Hornby)

'Mother knitting at
Dalton Hall', 1872
(watercolour by Victoria
Susan Hornby)

Dalton Hall, July 2014 – 'the stately doll's house'

The new hall, to the Clough Williams-Ellis design and said to be his last completed commission before his death in 1978, was completed in 1972.

Pevsner described the new house as 'a stately doll's house' which 'sits inside the ghost of its predecessor'.

The walls of the old entrance hall were retained up to waist level as a pleasing surround to what has now become a courtyard garden, the only hint of its former life being a hole in the stonework where the front door bell had once been.

The surrounding estate buildings now form a business complex and commercial centre. The estate also provides 'green funerals'. The Mason-Hornbys still occupy the 'new' hall and when I visited in 2014 they were able to identify various garden features shown in Victoria Susan's watercolours which correspond with those enjoyed to the present day. They were not much aware of the connection of the old hall with Lettie's grandmother, Victoria Susan Satterthwaite (nee Hornby).

Entrance steps to earlier Dalton Hall

CHAPTER FOUR

Dalton Hall influence, the Living at Disley and yet more good connections

It is doubtful if Lettie or her mother ever cooked. Maud was known to boil a pan of milk in the kitchen at Stonehurst but that is as far as her cooking was thought to have gone.

Lettie's interest in the kitchen was to decree that no tinned food was to be brought into the house. Of course, this decree was ignored but the daily cook was alive to the storm that would ensue if a tin was discovered so took care that the evidence was hidden and taken home. Miss Rogers, who cooked for Lettie for a short time, was always amused at Lettie's partiality for 'her' tomato soup, little knowing that it came from a Heinz tin!

But why should Mrs Satterthwaite or any of her daughters cook? They were not interested. They had other things to do and, in any event, their upbringing suggested that there was always someone to do the cooking. Their grandmother had been no different.

When Victoria Susan Hornby married Charles James Satterthwaite ('Charlie') on Tuesday 22 January 1861, she being aged 24 and her husband aged 30, the newly married couple moved to Banes Head Farm, Disley, before moving to Disley Parsonage, which was in the course of extension and alteration. Even there they had a cook. Victoria Susan brought Ellen Bramwell, aged 40, with her from Burton in Lonsdale near Dalton, having interviewed her in October 1860 and (so her diary reveals) 'found her to be very respectful'. No comment as to whether or not she could cook!

Later census returns continue to show the presence of a cook at Disley Parsonage. So Mrs Satterthwaite (Lettie's mother) would have been brought up on the basis that there was always a cook in the kitchen and indeed

Disley Vicarage, 1905

that was the case when she herself was married and living in the South.

Besides, as mentioned, there were other things to do. Victoria Susan's diaries show that before her marriage she enjoyed a full and vigorous life.

She played croquet, she took part in archery competitions with her brother Edmund, she 'played billiards with Papa', she went walking, she went out in 'the dog cart with Mama', she strummed the harmonium ('not very well'), she spent time doing 'my work' (needlework) and she had her painting. She also travelled abroad.

There were also numerous trips to Lancaster, particularly as her wedding approached, and also the 'disagreeable task' of signing the various documents relating to her marriage settlement and the financial matters that this entailed.

In short, she lived the comfortable life of a young woman in a well placed nineteenth-century family. She probably concerned herself little with domestic matters and doubtless her daughter, Lettie's mother Gertrude, was brought up in the same mould. In the next generation, Lettie and her sisters found they had enough to keep them occupied without being bothered by the inconvenience of the kitchen.

It is interesting to learn from the diaries of Victoria Susan of her courtship. She seemed to be constantly concerned as to her fiancé's health. She also showed a worldly interest in the declining health of Reverend Noble Wilson, at the time the incumbent of St. Mary's, Disley.

Charlie Reading *The Times*, Disley Parsonage 1879, a watercolour by Victoria Susan Satterthwaite (VSS)

It was acknowledged that Rev. Wilson was dying and that Charlie was to take his place, but there was obvious uncertainty as to the timing! In the event, Rev. Noble died on 9 October 1859 aged 63.

This was the signal to enable Charlie to arrange his wedding, subject to his appointment to the Living of Disley by the church patron.

Nothing so much as a chaste kiss from 'Charlie' is mentioned in the diaries and the diaries cease on the night before her wedding implying that she thinks it would be proper that she should cease to write a diary!

She had not always been so proper. Before her engagement to Charles James Satterthwaite it seems that she was affianced to a shoemaker, a very prosperous shoemaker but a shoemaker none the less. For a family of independent means and so well connected, this was not quite what was to be expected for a daughter of the Hornbys of Dalton Hall.

That she was allowed to be engaged to a shoemaker suggests a great deal of determination on Victoria Susan's part and resigned indulgence on the part of her father.

As her great uncle wrote to her mother in November 1859, 'what a horror. Poor Mundo, what a shock to all his aristocratic ideas ... what a little hussy ... all this comes of foreign travel ... what a dreadful example to set to Charlotte [her elder unmarried sister] ... If Miss Waller [the former governess] had but been on the spot this never could have happened – a trusty guardian and vigilant'.

In spite of his obvious relief at the new engagement, the great uncle took the opportunity to berate his great niece for 'having cruelly trifled with the feelings (let alone the fruit and the grapes?) of a most excellent man', the former fiancé. But he does go on to wish Victoria Susan well although complaining that the name 'Mrs Satterthwaite' does not trip easily off the tongue. He also hints at her strong character by remarking that 'you sign yourself Miss Victoria Susan Hornby in a bold character perhaps somewhat indicative of your disposition'

It is not surprising that Lettie was certainly of the same determined mould as her grandmother, as narrated in later chapters.

One suspects that as the wife of the Vicar of Disley Victoria Susan brought more than a whiff of glamour to the post. Charlie's family, as we shall see, was not without position in Lancaster, but his wife as the great niece of the powerful Earl of Derby was infinitely better connected. She was also obviously lively and a gifted watercolourist.

The Living at Disley was in the gift of the Legh family of nearby Lyme Hall, now a National Trust property. The

Lyme Hall, Disley (the South Front), the seat of the Legh Family. Jarrold Publishing, 1990

St. Oswald's Church, Winwick, Newton-le-Willows (2018)

aristocratic connection of Charlie's proposed wife would not have been lost on the Leghs, and could even have induced his appointment as vicar. But there were other historical links as well.

Geoffrey Hornby, Victoria Susan's great grandfather (1750–1812), had served as Sheriff and Lieutenant Colonel of the Lancashire militia in the 1770s. He had, so it is said, then taken Holy Orders to enjoy the rich proceeds of the rectory of Winwick, in the gift of the Stanleys. It helped, as we have seen, that he had married Lady Lucy Stanley (sister of the 12th Earl of Derby) in 1772!

He occupied the position of Rector from 1781 until his death in 1812.

It was said that the living of Winwick, St. Oswald's Church, being near to Knowsley Hall, was the best in the land. Some idea of its size is given by the fact that the Rector's son, Reverend John James Hornby (1777–1855) who succeeded him, divided the ancient parish covering 26,000 acres into 15 modern parishes.

It is fascinating to note that his successor, Rev. J. Hopwood (died 1890) married Lady Eleanor Stanley, sister of the 14th Earl of Derby, thus keeping a close connection between Winwick Church and its patron. But then, in those days, connections meant everything. Rev. Frank Hopwood became

Admiral Sir Geoffrey Thomas Phipps Hornby (in retirement) at his seat of Lordington, Sussex

Rector of Winwick and was the cousin of Admiral Sir Geoffrey Thomas Phipps Hornby who is mentioned later.

One might have thought that there was unlikely to be any connection between the Leghs of Lyme Hall, the owners of Dalton Hall and the parish of Winwick. But, there were.

The Lancashire and Cheshire Record Society in commenting on the parish of Burton in Kendal says that the manor of Dalton was assigned to Piers Legh of Lyme in 1489. It descended in that family until the death of Peter Thomas Legh in 1797, when it went to his sisters. It was sold to Rev. Geoffrey Hornby, the Rector of Winwick, in 1803. As we have seen, it was Rev. Hornby who founded the dynasty of Hornbys at Dalton Hall.

There is the further fascination that St. Oswald's Church at Winwick (known always as Winwick Church) contains 'The Legh Chapel' being a chantry chapel of the Legh family. A 'chantry' is broadly speaking an endowment for the singing or saying of Mass for the soul of the founders or persons named by them.

Land at Dalton was in 1539 charged to provide an income for the maintenance of this chapel and also to provide a chantry at Disley. The Abolition of Chantries Acts of 1545 and 1547 (at the time of the dissolution of the monasteries) would have removed these obligations.

So, if the Leghs did not know the Satterthwaites, they would certainly be aware of Charles's wife's family, the Hornbys. In short, Charles

Library interior at Lyme Hall, Cheshire 1871 (watercolour by VSS)

Satterthwaite provided all that might be expected of a nineteenth-century clergyman appointed by a nearby powerful family.

The walls at Stonehurst displayed many naval pictures and this puzzled me; Lettie had never referred by name to any naval connections. However, a little research revealed most distinguished naval forebears, albeit somewhat removed.

I have mentioned earlier the Rector of Winwick, Rev. Geoffrey Hornby, and his eldest son, Edmund, who married Lady Charlotte Smith Stanley, and from whom the Dalton Hall dynasty descended.

The Rector was a prolific breeder, siring 13 children, eight sons and five daughters. One of the sons, a brother to Edmund, rose high in the ranks of the Royal Navy.

This was Admiral Sir Phipps Hornby (1785–1867), as he became. He is commemorated at Winwick Church for his naval victory in the Adriatic against the French at the Battle of Lissa in 1811. A captured French flag is on display in the church having been presented by Captain Phipps Hornby, as he then was, to his father, the Rector.

Charlie writing his sermon at Disley Parsonage, 1879 (watercolour by Victoria Susan Satterthwaite)

The Rector must have been delighted by his son's success. He organised a party in his son's honour. The church booklet records that the inside of the Winwick Oak tree (alas, no longer standing) was 'covered with a fine white cloth, giving the appearance of a huge tent ... covering an area 100 yards in circumference' – quite some party!

The admiral in his turn provided the Royal Navy with another distinguished officer. Admiral Sir Geoffrey Thomas Phipps Hornby (1825–95) became President of the Royal Naval College at Greenwich in 1881 and Commander in Chief of the Royal Navy in 1882, retiring three years later.

This admiral showed an anxiety which was to be mirrored by his Satterthwaite relations nearly 100 years later. He confided to his diary on 31 December 1887 'So ends a year where ... I have experienced the most crushing anxiety and pinching for want of money'. This did not stop him however hunting and shooting at his estate at Lordington, near Chichester, West Sussex.

To complete a brief description of this distinguished service family, one should mention the three sons of Admiral Sir Geoffrey; firstly there was Captain Geoffrey Stanley Phipps Hornby (1856–1927) who was one of the earliest English polo players and who, on retiring from the army, became joint owner and manager of the Compton Stud at Gillingham, Dorset.

His brother, Brigadier General Edward John Phipps Hornby (1857–1947) won distinction in the Boer War, receiving the Victoria Cross and several other decorations.

The third son, Robert Stewart Phipps Hornby (1866–1956) joined the Royal Navy at the age of 13 and rose to be Admiral and Commander in Chief of the Royal Navy in the North America and West Indies Section.

This amazing line up was followed by Colonel Geoffrey Hardinge Phipps Hornby CBE (1889–1967), educated at Eton and Sandhurst, who, as well as his army career, was an accomplished point-to-point and polo player.

By way of contrast, James John Hornby (1826–1909), brother of Admiral Sir Geoffrey and another grandson of The Rector, was Headmaster of Eton College from 1868 until 1884, and subsequently Provost until his death in 1909. He was a distinguished rower.

I had always wondered why there was a picture of an Eton headmaster on the top landing at Stonehurst; research into this Hornby family provided the relationship but how or why the picture got there is impossible to say.

It turned out that there were other admiralty connections but we shall come to those later.

That the appointment to the Living at Disley of Charles James Satterthwaite as its vicar was obviously viewed as most suitable by its patron. This is evidenced by the paintings by Victoria Susan of members of the Legh family and of the interiors at Lyme Hall to which clearly she was allowed access. Rev. Charles Satterthwaite was Vicar of Disley for nearly 50 years.

The Satterthwaite ladies in Buxton could be justly proud of their forebears if ever they could sort out who was whom! But whichever way you look at it, they could justly say that they were 'well connected'. This was through their maternal grandmother Victoria Susan.

This is not to say that their maternal grandfather, Rev. Charles James Satterthwaite, had a pedigree without interest. This is of a different sort and is the subject of my next chapter.

CHAPTER FIVE

The Dark Secret

So whilst the antecedents of the maternal grandmother were now clear, I wanted to ascertain if Lettie could also claim to be 'well connected' through her maternal grandfather, Rev. Charles James Satterthwaite.

He was Vicar of Disley for nearly fifty years, he was a graduate of Jesus College, Cambridge, and he had been privately educated. This, for the time, suggested a family of note.

From Victoria Susan's diaries and her marriage certificate, it was apparent that 'Charlie' came from Lancaster. He had been curate at High Lane, between Disley and Stockport, before his appointment to Disley and had had the opportunity to view the prospects at Disley.

The patrons of the Living of Disley had also had the opportunity to assess the suitability of Rev. Satterthwaite as a successor to Rev. Wilson before they appointed him as Vicar.

How Charlie had come to this part of Derbyshire/Cheshire in the first place is not known. There were no apparent connections other than possibly through the influence of the Hornbys. As we have seen, the Leghs and the Hornbys had connections with Winwick Church and the Leghs had owned Dalton before its sale to Rev. Geoffrey Hornby. Could there have been a suggestion by Mundo Hornby to the Leghs that Disley might be a satisfactory Living for his potential son-in-law?

Victoria Susan's diaries reveal that whilst at High Lane Charlie was solicitous in enquiring about the health of the incumbent Vicar of Disley, Rev. Noble Wilson, who was known to be unwell. He died in office in October 1859 aged 63. Charlie was his successor.

Victoria Susan's watercolours show the Disley Parsonage to be well appointed and it had been either been newly built or refurbished before she moved in. But it is doubtful if it was her money alone that made that possible.

Kinder from the garden, Disley Vicarage, 3 September 1891
(a watercolour by Victoria Susan Satterthwaite)

When Charlie died in June 1910 aged 76, he left the goodly estate of £52,492. He had not inherited capital from his wife who had died in 1906. We know from Victoria Susan's diary that she was the beneficiary of a Marriage Settlement made at the time of her marriage and which, if this followed the usual form, would provide her with an income during her lifetime and which would have been paid to Charlie following her death. The capital would have gone to the children on his demise. There is no indication as to the size of this trust fund.

The size of Charlie's estate was not the sort of capital that could be amassed by being the Vicar of Disley and suggested that he must have had family money. Investigation as to how he might have come by it was revealing.

As the 'Who was Who 1897–1916' revealed, Charlie was one of the sons of James Cornelius Satterthwaite of Lancaster. The 1841 Census showed him to be living at Castle Hill, Lancaster, around the corner from the Hornbys at Castle Park, also in the proximity of the Castle. In that Census which revealed a household of himself, his wife, six children and four servants, James Cornelius described himself as 'of independent means'.

He was obviously of some local importance being a magistrate and, like Mundo Hornby, a Deputy Lord Lieutenant of the County. But how had he come by his good fortune?

St Helen's Church, Overton (July 2014)

A visit to Overton, outside Morecambe, and a few miles from Lancaster, was to lead me to the answer.

I knew of the connection between Overton and the Satterthwaites because Lettie's Will gave £500 to the Vicar and Churchwardens of Overton Church for the maintenance of the graveyard with the request that attention be given to the Satterthwaite graves and that of her Uncle Charles Geoffrey Satterthwaite. So to Overton I went.

Before I deal with my findings there, it is appropriate to emphasise how important Lancaster was in the late eighteenth and nineteenth centuries.

Lancaster gained its first charter in 1193 as a market town and borough. Its castle was originally built in 1164 and the Priory and Parish Church was built in the fifteenth century, although a priory founded in 1094 had preceded it. It was therefore a well established centre.

Lancaster is 208 miles from London. It dominated the surrounding area and indeed until 1835 Lancaster Castle was the only assize court in the entire county notwithstanding the growth of the industrial cities of Manchester and Liverpool.

Many buildings in the city centre and along St. George's Quay date from the eighteenth and early nineteenth centuries. The Custom House was built in 1764, the Grand Theatre in 1781 and the then Town Hall in 1783.

These and other buildings were constructed during a period when the port of Lancaster was one of the busiest in the UK. In 1722 22 ships arrived in Lancaster from overseas. By 1779 the number was 64.

Shipbuilding also took place at Lancaster. The Brockbank family yard built over 54 ships between 1779 and 1801. By 1830 shipbuilding had finished.

The port itself was served by the River Lune, which gave direct access to the sea. There were two landing points nearer the sea, towards the mouth of the river, being Sunderland Point and Bazil, the nearest village to which is Overton (see Map at Appendix, p.104).

Sunderland Point, on the north bank of the River Lune, served ships too large to sail up to the city. Bazil was a much smaller landing place.

The main trade of Lancaster was with the West Indies. Hardware and woollen goods were exported and sugar, rum and cotton formed a return cargo, in addition to mahogany which came into prominence through the furniture business of Robert Gillow, established in Lancaster.

The dominance of Lancaster only lasted for a short period as the River Lune began to silt up. Trade was lost to Glasson Dock, which lies near

Lancaster Castle (2019)

to the point where the river branches into the sea, and which opened in 1787. Glasson Dock, on the south side of the River Lune, was much more sheltered than the exposed Sunderland Point. In addition, it had access to the Lancaster to Preston Canal.

But neither Lancaster nor Glasson Dock could compete with Liverpool and its better facilities. In 1802 there were 42 ships out of Lancaster connected to the Indies trade. By 1830 the number had dropped to six. By 1850 the Lancaster maritime trade was pretty well dead.

The visit to Overton was most worthwhile. It confirmed the Satterthwaite connection with Overton. Both Charles James Satterthwaite and his wife Victoria Susan are buried there, and so too is James Cornelius Satterthwaite, who was described as being of Lancaster and Bazil.

There was plenty of information in the churchyard and I left my name and address in the Visitors' Book, saying that I was interested in the Satterthwaite family. This resulted in a telephone call from Mr Andrew Johnson who said that his mother was a Satterthwaite, being a daughter of Benjamin Hughes Satterthwaite, another grandchild of James Cornelius.

I asked where the Satterthwaite money came from and he told me that the Satterthwaites of Lancaster had been engaged in trade.

This was not surprising given the prosperity of the merchant class of Lancaster in the nineteenth century, but I had never heard talk by the ladies in Buxton of any connection to trade. Their late father, as a Lloyds Underwriter and Insurance broker, was not a member of the landed gentry, but, so far as they were concerned, he had not been engaged in trade!

Sunderland Point, July 2017

But what sort of trade? Perhaps the Buxton ladies did not know, or if they did, they did not want to talk about it, for 'trade' might be considered rather undignified if one had landed and aristocratic connections.

It is reckoned that in the late-eighteenth century, Lancaster was the fourth most important port engaged in the UK's slave trade. Now that certainly would have been lucrative – great British fortunes were built on that. The Lascelles (Earls of Harewood), the Beckfords and the Penrhyns (of Penrhyn Castle, North Wales) were prominent beneficiaries, to name but a few.

The profit made from slavery was mainly by reason of the cheap labour that slavery provided in the sugar plantations of the West Indies.

There is no evidence that the Satterthwaites were engaged in the slavery triangle – export of manufactured goods (guns, metalware etc.) to West Africa, collection of negroes from there to be used as slaves and transported in appalling conditions across the Atlantic to America and the West Indies to be sold, the ships returning to England laden with sugar, rum, molasses, cotton and timber.

But there is no doubt that the Satterthwaites profited from the slave trade. John Satterthwaite (1743–1807), the father of James Cornelius, married Mary (Polly) Stedman Rawlins of St. Kitts in 1777. Her father, Stedman Rawlins, was prominent there. He died in 1788.

An extract from his Will puts the possession of slaves into perspective; they were regarded as no more than chattels, just like a set of cutlery or tables and chairs:

'I desire that my executors do pay my daughter Mary, the wife of John Satterthwaite, Esquire of Lancaster, within six months after my decease the sum of five hundred pounds money unless the same be paid by myself during my lifetime in satisfaction of a parcel of negroes belonging to her and left in my possession when she quitted the island of St. Christopher' (the other name for St. Kitts).

Stedman Rawlins' Will, after the various bequests, left the remainder of his estate to his brother Joseph, his son Stedman, and his sons-in-law John Satterthwaite and James Akers. The size of his estate is not known, but we can assume that it was large in view of what is known of other plantation owners.

It is with some amusement that one notes one bequest in Stedman Rawlins' Will, one suspects by way of rebuke to his brother – he left him five guineas to purchase a mourning suit!

John Satterthwaite was clearly in a substantial way of business. His letter book covering the period 1764 to 1782 (and now in the possession of the University of Lancaster) sets out details of the cargoes sent out from Lancaster to St. Kitts – herrings, butter, beef, pork and cheese (all presumably well salted to preserve them!) – and the return cargoes of sugar, rum and cotton.

His father, Benjamin Satterthwaite (1718–92), had been agent for Robert Gillow, the founder of the cabinet making company, and it is probable that this agency continued with the son and Gillow's successors.

These voyages were not without risk. The Letter Book notes John Satterthwaite's concern about American privateers. On occasion his ship's departure was delayed because of privateers outside in the bay and he decided to wait until the arrival of the Royal Navy which would allow for a safe passage on departure.

The ship's cargo was often a partnership venture, thus spreading the risk of any potential loss. The sums concerned are substantial, one cargo alone being valued at £10,229, an incredible sum for that time.

However, such trading was highly profitable. John's clerk, John Stout, wrote that his master made 'a large part of his fortune' as a merchant in Lancaster between 1779 and 1785 so that he was able to retire in 1788.

John Satterthwaite was thus a prominent merchant in Lancaster. His portrait by the celebrated artist George Romney (*c*.1780) hangs in the Judges' Lodgings

John Satterthwaite, *c*.1780, portrait by George Romney, in the Judge's Lodgings Museum, Lancaster, on loan from Mr Giles Johnson.

in Lancaster. This is surely an illustration of his stature in the city. He died on Boxing Day 1807.

By then any slave trading which involved shipping by a Lancaster merchant had ceased. Legislation of 1799 decreed that slaving ships could only sail from Liverpool, London and Bristol. Lancaster merchants were thus limited to trading other products and goods although Lancaster investments in the Slave Trade could still continue from Liverpool.

The Slave Trade Act of 1807 outlawed the purchasing of Africans in the British Empire but slavery itself in the British Colonies was not abolished until the Slave Abolition Act of 1833. Even then a system of apprenticeships meant that in practice slavery did not finish until August 1840.

Compensation was paid to slave owners as they were losing 'their property'. The British Government raised £20 Million (about £69 billion in 2013 pounds) to pay compensation to the registered owners of freed slaves. The University College of London in its project 'Legacies of British Slave Ownership' lists the Rawlins family as receiving various sums. These fall far short of the £26,309 received by the 2nd Earl of Harewood for one plantation, but it is clear that they benefitted.

As we shall see from the next chapter, John Satterthwaite was a very rich man and divided his estate between his children. One way or another therefore it is not surprising that James Cornelius Satterthwaite, Lettie's great grandfather, was financially well placed. Victoria Susan's diary records 'Mr Satterthwaite' (being James Cornelius) 'at the window of his counting house'. This suggests that James Cornelius, like his father, was a merchant.

In 1837, his nephew was writing that 'Uncle James is still down at Sunderland', no doubt supervising some shipping. By 1839 he was acquiring over 50 acres of land at Bazil Point, together with 16 acres of land at Overton. The Bazil Point land was particularly valuable as it was suitable for quarrying and, as the Auction Particulars make clear, 'it is accessible to vessels of 50 to 60 tons burden and is conveniently situate for shipping stones'.

So, although he was survived by six children, the mercantile activity of his father, who was himself assisted by a substantial inheritance, helps to explain the financial prosperity of Charles James Satterthwaite when he died in 1910.

Lettie would never have known her great grandfather as James Cornelius died in 1857. Her maternal grandfather, 'Charlie', was a clergyman and one can surmise that this that is why possibly 'the Dark Secret' of the Slave Trade, or indeed trade at all, was never mentioned.

Research into this family continued to throw up fascinating facts. The larger family tree shows up a plethora of Anglican clergymen. I was surprised therefore to discover that Benjamin Satterthwaite, the father of John Satterthwaite, was brought up as a Quaker. However by marrying Jane, the daughter of Alderman John Casson of Lancaster, an Anglican, and the marriage taking place in an Anglican church, Benjamin was disowned by the Society of Friends on 5 October 1741. Long term, it does not seem to have done the Satterthwaite financial interests any harm!

At this stage, Lettie's maternal family has been ascertained. She had the good connections, through her mother, albeit somewhat distant, to the Hornbys of Dalton Hall and to the Stanleys. Her maternal grandmother, Victoria Susan, became a Satterthwaite on marrying Rev. Charles James Satterthwaite, and thus Lettie's mother Gertrude was a Satterthwaite at the time of her own marriage to John Sheridan Satterthwaite.

So if Lettie's father was a Satterthwaite, was he too related to the Satterthwaites of Lancaster? It was time to investigate Lettie's paternal forbears.

Before we do so let us just side-track a little to mention Sambo's Grave and Fanny's Hand, both stories giving a little flavour of Lancaster's close connection with the Slave Trade.

It also gives us a chance to look at Robert Gillow, the well known cabinet and furniture maker.

A little aside – Sambo's Grave and Fanny's Hand

It is impossible to read about the Slave Trade as it affected Lancaster, without seeing mention of Sambo.

Sunderland Point, already mentioned, houses a very small community, then as now. It is only accessible via a narrow road, which crosses a soft marsh, and is cut off at high tide. For these reasons the establishment of Glasson Dock in 1787, on the opposite side from the entrance to the sea of the River Lune, hastened its decline as a landing point.

But in 1736 it was a flourishing port.

According to the Lonsdale Magazine of 1822, Sambo had arrived around 1736 from the West Indies as a servant to the captain of an un-named ship.

Further to this sad story, Sambo was left at a nearby inn to await his master's return from elsewhere. Presumably his master would have gone to Lancaster to negotiate the sale of his newly arrived cargo and to purchase goods for the return journey to the West Indies.

Signpost to Sambo's Grave at Sunderland Point

Sambo obviously did not understand what he might have been told. Poor Sambo, thinking that he had been deserted by his master in this strange land 'fell into a complete state of stupefaction', settled down in the loft of the nearby brewhouse and refused all sustenance. Naturally enough he died, whether from lack of food and water or from an infection, is not known.

To continue to quote the magazine, 'As soon as Sambo's exit was known to the sailors who happened to be there, they excavated him a grave in a lonely dell in a rabbit warren behind the village, within twenty yards of the sea shore whither they conveyed his remains without either coffin or bier, being covered only with the clothes in which he died'.

Sambo was buried in unconsecrated ground as it was not known if he was a Christian.

The story became known to a schoolmaster, Rev. James Watson, and in or about 1796 he raised money for a memorial to be placed on the unmarked grave. The grave is now a popular tourist attraction.

Rev. Watson penned a few words which appealed to his Georgian audience:

Full sixty years the angry winter's wave
Has thundering dashed this bleak and barren shore
Since Sambo's head laid in this lonely grave
Lies still and ne'er will hear their turmoil more.

Full many a sandbird chirps upon the sod
And many a moonlight elfin round him trips
Full many a summer's sunbeam warms the clod
And many a teeming cloud upon him drips.

But still he sleeps – till the awakening sounds
Of the Archangel's trump new life impart
Then the Great Judge his approbation founds
Not on man's colour but his worth of heart.

This tale does illustrate that it was not unusual for the merchants of Lancaster to have a black servant and, as Hugh Cunliffe mentions in his booklet on Sunderland Point, 'it became fashionable to have a negro servant and many of the big houses in the Lune Valley would have had them'.

Indeed, it would appear that John Satterthwaite had one such. The Lancaster Priory Church Records show that on 2 April 1778 Frances Elizabeth Johnson (Fanny), a black woman servant of John Satterthwaite, was baptised in The Priory.

It is not known when Fanny died or where she was buried. There is the macabre story that her hand was passed down through generations of the family before being buried in The Priory Memorial Garden, with soil from St. Kitts, in 1997.

It is said that the retention of the hand for so long was a reminder of a much treasured and loved servant, whose hand gave comfort to lonely members of the family. It apparently hung for many years above the fireplace at 20, Castle Park, Lancaster, the Satterthwaite family home for several generations.

(Full details behind this story can be found on the internet 'Fanny's Hand – Castle Park Stories')

Robert Gillow (1704–1772)

Waring and Gillow

I MENTION THE ABOVE as the name of Gillow is synonymous with Lancaster. Given the connection between Robert Gillow and the Satterthwaites, a brief account of his business might be of interest.

It is thought that having served an apprenticeship as a joiner and cabinet maker, Robert Gillow sailed on a Satterthwaite ship to the West Indies as a ship's carpenter.

He became aware of mahogany and brought samples back to Lancaster, founding the firm which became known as 'Gillows of Lancaster' in 1730.

Lancaster records show that Gillow and his associates employed Benjamin Satterthwaite (1718–1792) as factor in Barbados between 1749 and 1751. It is probable that this agency continued with Benjamin's son, John Satterthwaite, and Gillow's successors.

In his early years Robert Gillow fitted out ships' cabins and finalised construction works. It is probable that, in addition to importing mahogany, he also imported rum and sugar, as did most Lancaster merchants.

His firm rapidly established a reputation for supplying high quality furniture and a London branch of the business was set up on Oxford Street in 1764.

Gillow's two sons, Richard (1733–1811) and Robert (1745–93), joined the business and continued it after Robert Gillow's death in 1772. It was

Waring and Gillow, Oxford Street, London

really Richard who drove the business forward establishing the firm's reputation for producing good quality furniture at reasonable prices made by competent workmen from first class material.

Richard Gillow was the architect of the Customs House, Lancaster. He is also credited with originating the telescopic dining table, which he patented in 1800. He described his invention as 'calculated to reduce the number of legs and pillars and claws in the construction of dining and other tables and to facilitate and render easy their enlargement and reduction in size'.

A telescopic table can be seen at Leighton Hall, near Carnforth, Lancashire, the Gillow family seat after its purchase by another Richard Gillow (1772–1849), a grandson of the founder. The house contains other examples of Gillow furniture.

During the final years of the nineteenth century, the firm ran into financial difficulty; they found that they were competing against mass produced furniture which was obviously cheaper than bespoke items. Demand for Gillow furniture dropped. However support from Warings of Liverpool enabled them to continue. The combined business became Waring and Gillow in 1903.

Warings of Liverpool had been founded by John Waring from Belfast in 1835. He had established a wholesale cabinet making business. This business was expanded by his son, Samuel Jones Waring, with the firm furnishing hotels and public buildings. His building company (Waring White Building Company) built the Liverpool Corn Exchange, Selfridge's Department Store and the London Ritz Hotel. Warings were thus big business men dealing with large projects as opposed to bespoke items of furniture.

By 1932 the company of Waring and Gillow was registered as Waring and Gillow (1932) Limited. Its reputation for high quality furniture and cabinet making was enhanced by the fitting out of the royal yacht Victoria and Albert and the Queen Mary (1936) and Queen Elizabeth (1940) liners for Cunard.

Following the end of the Second World War, during which the upholstery department of the business was engaged in making kit-bags, tents and camouflage netting amongst other items, the business declined. The Lancaster workshops closed in 1962.

In 1980, Waring and Gillow joined with the cabinet making firm of Maple & Co to become Maple, Waring and Gillow. This was subsequently absorbed into Allied Carpets.

Chapter Six

In Chancery

Whilst Lettie's maternal forebears were quite clearly from Lancaster, in spite of the name it was not certain that her paternal forebears were from the same city, although it was likely. Certainly the name 'Satterthwaite' suggested that they were from the Lake District area.

I felt that the little enclave of Satterthwaite, some four miles from Hawkshead in the Lake District, might provide a lead. This enquiry was reinforced by seeing a booklet which contained a family tree showing Benjamin Satterthwaite as a son of Thomas Satterthwaite (1685–1728) of 'Hawkshead and Leeds'. No authority was given for this statement so I felt that a visit to the village of Satterthwaite might provide an answer.

It was not to be. The church, built in about 1840 to replace an earlier church which had been in existence since the sixteenth century, contained no mention of any Satterthwaite. The graveyard, recently surveyed and a full list of those interred there published, contained no mention of a Satterthwaite either.

This investigation was before I had discovered that Benjamin Satterthwaite and his forebears had been Quakers. It was not surprising therefore that there were no Satterthwaites in an Anglican churchyard.

However, nearby was a charming Quaker burial ground, established in 1691 or thereabouts, at Colthouse Town End. It transpired that Thomas Satterthwaite had once held property there. The graveyard revealed a few Satterthwaites, but not the ones I was looking for.

By this time it had become apparent to me that there were several branches of Satterthwaites devolving from Thomas Satterthwaite of Leeds and Hawkshead. I had to remind myself that I was not investigating the Satterthwaite family but merely trying to establish Lettie's paternal line.

I was pretty certain that Lettie's paternal family was descended from John Satterthwaite of Lancaster, but it was a question of ascertaining hard fact.

The clue was probably in the name of 'Sheridan'; Lettie's father had been called John [Arthur] Sheridan Satterthwaite and her paternal grandfather had been called Charles Sheridan Satterthwaite. He had been born in 1811.

I needed to explore further the descendants and affairs of John Satterthwaite.

I have mentioned that John Satterthwaite died on 26 December 1807. His wife, Mary Stedman (nee Rawlins), the daughter of the plantation owner in St. Kitts, survived him by almost 30 years. There were eleven children of the marriage, of whom James Cornelius Satterthwaite was the youngest (born 2 September 1798). He, as we have seen, was Lettie's great grandfather on her maternal side.

The longevity of his mother, combined with the terms of John Satterthwaite's Will, were to cause a problem. It was the sorting out of that problem however that was to provide the pointer to Lettie's paternal background.

John Satterthwaite's Will of 20 May 1797 left his house at Castle Hill, Lancaster, together with the stables, gardens and coachhouse to his wife, Mary so long as she wished to live there. She continued to do so. There was no difficulty with this bequest.

A corner of the Quaker Burial Ground at Colthouse Town End, Hawkshead (2019)

He left £4,000 to each of his five sons and £2,500 to each of his four daughters, a son and a daughter having predeceased their father without leaving issue. These legacies, totalling £30,000, also caused no difficulty. They merely indicated the size of a very satisfactory estate, the legacies alone being worth in total something in the order of £2 million today.

It would appear that there were difficulties in establishing what exactly was comprised in the estate. John Satterthwaite owned various properties outright but had interests in other properties and enterprises. Whilst certain property assets were charged to provide for an annuity of £400 per annum for the widow, there were also directions to provide for the education of children and deal with surplus income. Subject to these and other provisions, the estate was left equally amongst John Satterthwaite's children. Any deceased child's share was to pass to their respective children.

As early as June 1813 proceedings about the estate had occurred when a decree in Chancery had ordered that an Account be taken of John Satterthwaite's estate he 'being at the time of his death seised and possessed of considerable real and personal estate'. In other words, what exactly had John Satterthwaite owned at the time of his death.

By 1830, not only was the residuary estate producing £1,671 per annum, but several children had died. Other children had settled their prospective interests in trust by way of marriage settlement.

Administering the estate must have become increasingly difficult. The properties had to be managed, Mary had to be paid her annuity, and the surplus income had to be dealt with. The costs would be high. In addition, the estate's assets were illiquid and might no longer be suitable investments.

If sales were made, the £400 per annum required for Mary could be found by investing sufficient of the sale proceeds in the purchase of Government securities of an amount required to produce this income. This would enable the balance of the estate to be distributed.

Because some of those interested in the estate were infants, it was necessary for the Court to sanction any arrangements as obviously an infant is not legally of age to give consent to any change. A similar position would apply today.

It is not necessary here to go into the nineteenth-century intricacies of trust law nor how applications to amend the terms of a will, bearing in mind the associated time limits, should be made.

The end result was a Petition to the House of Lords (2 Geo IV Session 1821) for a Parliamentary Bill to be passed 'to enable the surviving trustee under the Will of John Satterthwaite deceased to sell the real estate thereby

2 GEO. IV. **3° Aprilis.**

Satterthwaite et al. Leave to present a Petition for a Bill:

Upon reading the Petition of *Mary Satterthwaite* Widow, on behalf of herself and as the personal Representative of *Anne Armett* deceased; *Rawlins Satterthwaite, William Hopes,* and *William Bell,* as personal Representatives of *William Fawcett,* deceased; *Benjamin Satterthwaite, James Cornelius Satterthwaite, John Bolden* and *Mary* his Wife, and *Elizabeth Postlethwaite,* on their own Behalves respectively, and the said *John Bolden* as surviving Trustee in the Indenture of Settlement made in Contemplation of the Marriage of *Cæsar Colclough Armett* and the said *Ann Armett,* both deceased; *Robert Michaelson* and *Millicent* his Wife, on Behalf of themselves and *Thomas Yeates Parker Michaelson, Robert Henry Machell Michaelson, Millicent Lucinda Michaelson, Charles Williams Michaelson,* and *John Frederick Satterthwaite Michaelson,* their Infant Children; and the said *Millicent Michaelson* as personal Representative of *Charles Satterthwaite,* deceased; and the said *Robert Michaelson* as personal Representative of *Frances Nannette Georgiana Satterthwaite,* also deceased, the Wife of the said *Charles Satterthwaite,* and as the Guardian of *Charles Sheridan Satterthwaite* and *Francis Neynoe Satterthwaite,* the Infant Children of the said *Charles Satterthwaite* and *Frances Nannette Georgiana Satterthwaite;* setting forth, " That *John Satterthwaite,* " formerly of *Lancaster,* in the County of *Lancaster,* " Esquire, being in his Life-time and at the Time of his " Death seized and possessed of considerable Real and " Personal Estates, did duly make and publish his last " Will and Testament, bearing Date the 20th Day of " *May* 1797, and thereby, after ordering and directing " that all his just Debts, Funeral Expences, and the " Legacies and Annuities therein-after given and be- " queathed, should be paid, he the said Testator gave and " devised his Dwelling House, in which he then dwelt, " with Two Stables, Two Coach-houses, and Two Gardens " thereunto belonging, being in the *Castle Hill,* in *Lan-* " *caster,* in the County of *Lancaster,* unto his dear " Wife *Mary Satterthwaite,* so long as she should continue " his Widow, and might choose to live and reside therein, " but no longer; but if she should rather choose, whilst " his Widow, to dwell and reside in any other Place, he " ordered and directed that she should have and be paid " the Sum of Fifty Pounds a year in the lieu of his House, " Stables, and Gardens in *Lancaster* aforesaid, in which " Case the said Premises might be let or sold by the " Trustees of his said Will, and the Rents and Profits " thereof applied by them as therein-after is directed as " to the Residue of his Estate, for the general Benefit " and Increase thereof; and the said Testator thereby " also gave to his said Wife, the Use of all the House- " hold Furniture, Linen, China, and Plate, during her " Life, and the Time she should continue his Widow, but " if she should continue his Widow 'till the Time of her " Decease, but not otherwise; the First Payment thereof " to begin and be made at the End of Six Calendar " Months next after his Decease; but if his said Wife " should marry again, then he thereby revoked and made " void the Devise or Bequest of the said Annuity of Four " hundred Pounds, which was from thenceforth to cease " and be no longer paid; and the said *James Topping, " John Stout,* and *Joseph Rawlins,* his said Trustees, and " the Survivors and Survivor of them, and the Heirs, " Executors, or Administrators of such Survivor, were " from thenceforth, in lieu thereof, to pay to his said Wife, " or her Assigns, or to permit and suffer her to receive, " out of the Rents and Profits of the said Premises, during " her Life, the clear yearly Annuity or Sum of Two hun- " dred Pounds, by equal Half-yearly Payments as aforesaid, " for her own sole and separate Use, free and clear from " all Taxes and Deductions whatsoever, for which her " Receipts alone, notwithstanding her Coverture, were " to be the only good and valid Discharges, and the same " was not to be liable to the Debts, Control, or Engage- " ments of any Husband she might thereafter intermarry " with; and the said Testator thereby declared, that the " Provision thereby made for his said Wife as aforesaid, " should be in lieu and satisfaction for her Dower or " Widow Right, and of all other Claims whatsoever in or " to his Real or Personal Estate; and the said Testator " thereby gave and bequeathed unto his Mother *Jane " Satterthwaite,* (who died in the Life-time of the said " Testator,) the yearly Annuity of Eighty Pounds, to be " paid Half-yearly during her Life, the first Payment " thereof to be made at the End of Six Calendar Months " after his Decease; and also to each of his Sons then " born, or thereafter to be born, the Sum of Four thou- " sand Pounds each, to be paid to them respectively by " the Executors of his said Will, out of his Personal " Estate, as they should respectively attain the Age of " Twenty-two Years; and he thereby also gave and be- " queathed unto each of his Daughters then born or " thereafter to be born, a Legacy or Sum of Two thousand " five hundred Pounds a-piece, to be paid to them, out of " his Personal Estate, as they should respectively attain " the Age of Twenty-one Years or Marriage, which " should first happen, provided such Marriage under the " Age aforesaid was with the Consent of the major Part " of the Trustees and Executors of his said Will; but if " such Marriage should be without the Consent afore- " said, then the said Testator ordered and directed that " the Bequests therein contained to her and them so " marrying under that Age, without such Consent afore- " said, should be void; and the said Testator not only " revoked the same, but ordered that the Portion and

Petition to the House of Lords 1821 (an extract)

devised during the lifetime of the Testator's widow and to pay the purchase monies into the Bank [of England] to be applied under the direction of the Court of Chancery'.

The application was 'greatly for the benefit of all parties interested in the estate' and would enable the residuary estate to be distributed.

There is no indication of the costs involved but they must have been very considerable.

One surmises the required sales were made and the monies lodged as directed and then distributed as the Chancery Court ordered. As to the amounts, there is a reference among the papers held by Lancashire Archives at Preston, that suggests that the share of each of John Satterthwaite's children in his estate in 1830 amounted to £13,666 (roughly equivalent to £820,000 each today). Together with his other monies, this would certainly confirm that James Cornelius Satterthwaite could properly be described as 'of independent means' in the 1841 Census. That monies were still in Chancery in 1830 puts one in mind of the case of Jarndyce and Jarndyce so vividly portrayed in Charles Dickens' Bleak House.

But it was the pre-amble to the Petition which was to give me valuable information. Apart from confirming the considerable size of John Satterthwaite's estate, by listing the lands he held, it confirmed the names of his children, one of whom was Charles Satterthwaite, born in 1786.

It also confirmed that this Charles Satterthwaite had died on 7 October 1815 without a Will and that his widow, Frances Nanette Georgiana Satterthwaite had died on 14 October 1816, leaving her estate to their two children, Charles Sheridan Satterthwaite and Francis Neynoe Satterthwaite, both then infants. Their aunt, Millicent Michaelson (nee Satterthwaite) a sister to James Cornelius, was to administer their affairs. She, and her husband Robert, are named as guardians of the two infants in the parliamentary proceedings.

I do not know the cause of death of Charles Satterthwaite who died at the age of only 29, nor of his wife who died aged 26. There was a hint, no more, that he might have drowned as was the fate of his sister Anne Armett, her husband and their three children, who died at sea when the Berwickshire packet travelling between England and Ireland went down on 24 January 1819.

Drowning seemed to be a hazard of the time as Frederick Postlethwaite (a grandson of John Satterthwaite) drowned in 1835 whilst crossing from Grange. It is a reminder that transport between places was often quicker by sea than by road.

But however Charles Satterthwaite died, I now had confirmation by way of the name Charles Sheridan Satterthwaite of Lettie's paternal grandfather, who was only four when his father died. This tallied with his known date of birth. He was a grandson of John Satterthwaite. So, both Lettie's maternal and paternal side were descended from the materially very successful John Satterthwaite. This could certainly account for monies within the family.

Why suddenly the name of 'Sheridan' had cropped up provided another mystery, and is the subject of the next chapter.

CHAPTER SEVEN

The Sheridan Connection and Paternal Grandpapa

MOST OF US WILL HAVE HEARD of Richard Brinsley Sheridan (1751–1816), the playwright and author of 'The School for Scandal'. But how were the Satterthwaites connected to this family?

To start with the only clues were in the names of Lettie's father, John Arthur Sheridan Satterthwaite, her paternal grandfather Charles Sheridan Satterthwaite, the small picture entitled 'the tomb of Mrs Charles Francis Sheridan' on the first floor landing at Stonehurst and the Johnson Dictionary.

This last item consisted of two mighty tomes kept in a cupboard under the bookcase in the dining room and bearing a leather bookplate saying it was a gift from the Author to Thomas Sheridan in 1755.

Research showed that Thomas Sheridan (1719–88), a godson of Jonathan Swift of *Gulliver's Travels* fame, had returned to England from Ireland in 1756, having made his debut on the Irish stage as an actor, written various plays and been manager of the Dublin theatre. He had been born in Dublin but educated in England until his father's financial problems forced the family to return to Ireland. The family could thus properly refer to themselves as Anglo-Irish.

The eldest child of Thomas Sheridan was Charles Francis Sheridan, born in 1750, the elder brother of the playwright.

These easily ascertained facts did not appear to be leading me to a Satterthwaite connection. But then it came from two sources.

First, a family tree of the Sheridans provided by the Samuel Johnson Birthplace Museum in Lichfield. This showed a daughter (unnamed) of Charles Francis Sheridan marrying 'Satterwaite', with no further details given.

Secondly, an internet cross reference to the descendants of Colonel Charles Lyons of Ledeston, Westmeath, Ireland (1690–1780), High Sheriff of Westmeath (1731). And, there it was; a marriage between his descendant Letitia Christiana Bolten to Charles Francis Sheridan. They had several children, one of whom, Frances Anna Georgiana Sheridan (1790–1816) and whom we shall call 'Georgiana Satterthwaite', married Charles Satterthwaite in or about 1811.

We know from the Petition to the House of Lords that Charles Satterthwaite was a son of John Satterthwaite and that he had married Georgiana and that they had two children one of whom was Charles Sheridan Satterthwaite, born in 1811.

By reason of that and the earlier cross references, the Satterthwaite connection to the Sheridan family could be explained, and Lettie's paternal forebears established.

It was by reason of the marriage of Georgiana Satterthwaite (nee Sheridan) to Charles Satterthwaite that the Johnson Dictionary referred to earlier passed down the Satterthwaite family; she inherited it by reason of being the eldest child of Charles Francis Sheridan.

Bookplate to Johnson Dictionary (1755)

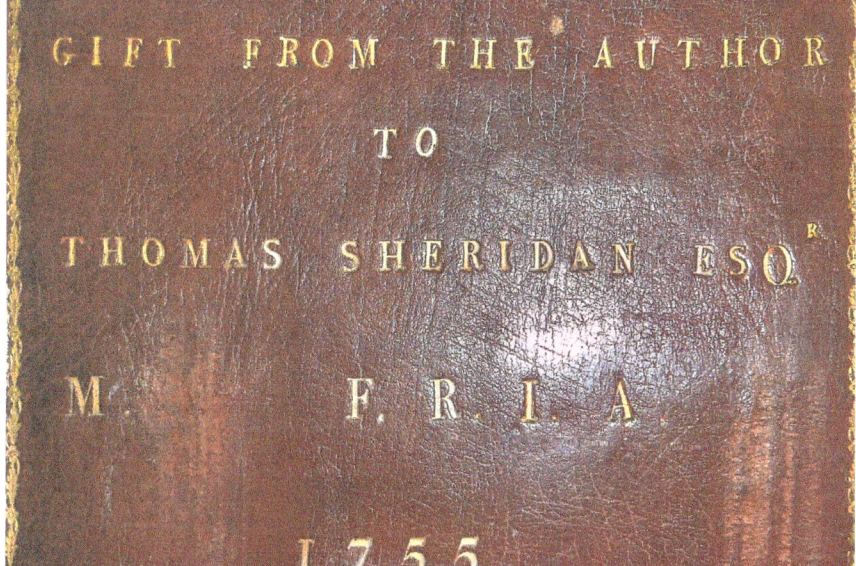

This connection would also explain the several eighteenth-century portraits in the dining room at Stonehurst, one of which was said to be attributed to William Hogarth (1697–1764) and to have been a gift from him to Thomas Sheridan. Unfortunately the identity of the subjects of these portraits remains unknown.

So there we have it – both Lettie's paternal side and her maternal side were descended from John Satterthwaite of Lancaster. Her father and her mother were second cousins as they had a common great grandfather (John Satterthwaite). Or, put another way, her paternal grandfather (whom we have not yet met other than by his name) and her maternal grandfather ('Charlie') were first cousins.

I was puzzled about Mrs Satterthwaite's strictures to her daughters about the dangers of cousins marrying cousins. This could not surely refer to her own marriage. That was a marriage of second cousins. The Hornby/Stanley first cousin marriages were a long time ago. Further research however gave an answer and also explained better the number of seascapes on the walls at Stonehurst and Lettie's offhand references to Admiralty connections.

Georgiana Satterthwaite (nee Sheridan) had a sister, Letitia Elizabeth Sheridan, who married John Gore Jones. There were seven children of that marriage of whom two are of relevance to the Satterthwaites. Let us look first at one of the sons.

The third son, William, rose to become Rear Admiral William Brydges Neynoe Gore-Jones. The hyphen in his name seemed to appear as he rose up the ranks of the Royal Navy; the other names appeared to come and go often depending upon the space on a page!

William Gore Jones was born in Ireland in 1826. By 1848 he was a Lieutenant in the Royal Navy receiving the French legion d'honneur (5th class) for his services in the Black Sea during the Crimean War. Promoted to Captain by 1861 he took command of HMS *Princess Royal* in 1864. By this time his first wife had died and he married Agnes Spankie, a lady with Scottish connections, who was born in Calcutta.

The East Indies Station of the Royal Navy was established in 1865 and served the Indian Ocean, the Persian Gulf and the Red Sea (excluding the waters round South Africa, Australia and certain waters round the Dutch East Indies). Gore-Jones (for the hyphen was now in use!) was appointed Commander in Chief, East Indies Station, in 1879 and served until 1882. It is interesting to read that on the night of 4 April 1881, whilst his ship *Euryalus* was moored in Bombay Harbour, the Rear Admiral was being comfortably looked after as he had a personal staff of a steward, cook and three domestics.

The rear admiral retired in 1887. He died the following year leaving an estate of £7,052. It may be that his wife had money of her own or there was a very generous navy pension scheme. Certainly she was comfortably placed for at the time of the 1911 Census, aged 89, she was living in an 18 roomed house in South Kensington with four servants to attend to her needs. She died in 1912. There were no children.

Lettie's Will refers to the paintings of 'Uncle William and his wife Agnes on either side of the serving table in my dining room' (actually they would have been Lettie's great uncle and aunt), so the admiralty connection is explained.

It is quite likely that Lettie would have visited the Rear Admiral's widow in Kensington whilst the Satterthwaites were living in Kenley.

So in addition to her aristocratic and landed gentry forebears, Lettie could quite justifiably point to her Admiralty connections – the somewhat distant Phipps Hornbys (ante pp. 31–3) and the Gore Joneses.

But we have another Gore Jones to deal with. Admiral William's sister, Arabella Louisa Gore Jones, born in 1830 in County Sligo, Ireland, had married the orphaned Charles Sheridan Satterthwaite at Thurles in County Tipperary, Ireland, in 1854. This was her first cousin as her mother Letitia Gore-Jones (née Sheridan) was the sister of Georgiana Satterthwaite (nee Sheridan).

The Gore Jones, like the Sheridans, were an Anglo-Irish family; the wedding, although it took place in strongly Catholic Ireland, did not mean that the Satterthwaites were about to embrace Roman Catholicism. Both families remained members of the established church. Ireland at that time was still part of the United Kingdom.

So many people in this little histoire seemed to marry into a related family that perhaps Mrs Satterthwaite was right to be concerned that her daughters should not do so. In spite of the close marriages, there is no suggestion that any offspring were 'not quite right'. And there is no other apparent reason why the girls should not marry.

The early life of Charles Sheridan Satterthwaite is vague. He was the only son of Charles Satterthwaite and Georgiana and was born in 1811 at Wavertree, Liverpool. His father Charles Satterthwaite had no doubt removed there as the fortunes of the port of Lancaster declined.

Nothing is known about Charles Sheridan Satterthwaite's schooling or early career, but he obviously decided that his fortune lay in London.

By 1830, his grandmother Mary Satterthwaite was writing to him from Castle Hill, Lancaster, and addressing her letter to him at Pickford & Co.,

Wood Street, London. So, by the age of 19 he was probably working for this large haulage firm who had embraced the emerging railway network as well as using horse drawn transport.

Confirmation of his connection to Pickfords comes from his Will in which he bequeathed 'my four silver candlesticks presented to me by Messrs. Pickford and Company' to his son John Sheridan Satterthwaite.

He was obviously regarded as respectable for he was appointed as a Special Constable on 8 April 1848 at a time when a large number of special constables were enrolling as the authorities were fearful of disturbances incited by the Chartist movement.

By 1851, when he was aged 40, he was living in lodgings near St. Pancras. He gave his occupation in the census of that year as a 'Rail Clerk'.

We have seen that he married his cousin Arabella Louisa Gore Jones in 1854. He must have prospered for the 1861 Census shows him living at Orsett Terrace, Paddington, London, where he is described as a 'railway clerk'. This description is a broad one as his household also consisted, apart from his wife Arabella and four children, of a cook, housemaid and two nursemaids. Although it was not uncommon to have servants, this does suggest a relatively comfortable household.

A later census described him as a Railway Agent. By the time of his death in 1897 aged 86 he was described as a gentleman and was living at Lancaster Lodge, Putney Park Avenue, London SW15, a good address not far from Barnes Common. He left a satisfactory estate of £20,968. His wife, Arabella, survived him, dying in 1902.

These were Lettie's paternal grandparents. As she was born in 1895 she probably had little memory of them and indeed little memory of her maternal grandparents who had died in 1906 and 1910 respectively at a time when the family was still living in Kenley.

Charles Sheridan Satterthwaite's estate included shares in Thames Steam Tug and Lighterage Company Limited.

The connection with transport might account for some of the effects at Stonehurst on Lettie's death in 1986 and for her sizeable shareholding in Transport Development Group plc, a transport holding company.

Although her father had been a Lloyds Underwriter and Insurance Broker, he was also a shareholder in Thames Steam Tug and Lighterage Co. Limited, probably inherited from his father. He may also have been a Director of the company.

A Lighter was used to convey goods from ship to shore when there was no closed dock available. In the early days of the nineteenth century, power was provided by man power. With the advent of steam, a small tug could be used to tow several lighters. If they were to go to wharves above London Bridge, steam tugs were fitted with funnels that folded down.

The Thames and General Lighterage Co. Ltd, which encompassed Thames Steam Tug and Lighterage Co. Ltd., issued its prospectus on 9 July 1856 with a capital of £200,000 offering for sale 20,000 shares of £10 each. By 1904 the company owned 340 barges and five tugs. It was therefore a fairly substantial company.

Mr Satterthwaite, Lettie's father, must have had a closer connection with the company than that of a mere shareholder for they built two tugs named after two of his children.

The tug 'Maud' was built in 1900. A rather poor photograph shows its launching and one of the children is probably Maud, then aged 9. A subsequent aquatint gives a rather better picture.

I had always been charmed by this picture and when Lettie offered to leave me a picture in her Will, this is what I chose – to her disapproval as will become apparent.

The tug 'Maud' was sold by Thames Steam Tug and Lighterage in 1929 and scrapped in 1954.

Launching of the Tug *Maud* (1900)

The tug 'Lettie' had a rather more adventurous life. She was built in Rotterdam in 1914 and delivered to Thames Steam that year only to be requisitioned in 1916 for admiralty service at Harwich, returning to her owners in 1919. She was requisitioned again in 1940 to serve as an auxiliary patrol vessel only to be lost off St. Abb's Head, Scotland in November 1941, cause unknown. Her crew are remembered on the Merchant Navy Memorial at Tower Hill, London.

In 1961, the Company was employing over 400 lightermen, but times were difficult and the company accepted a takeover bid of £780,000 from Transport Development Group. They sold on this division to William Cory Limited in 1980.

So now Lettie's ancestry has become clear. She was well connected – the Stanleys and the Hornbys. She had trading connections, even if not acknowledged – the Satterthwaites of Lancaster, Liverpool and London. She had admiralty connections – the Phipps Hornby and Gore Jones forebears – and she had Irish ancestry through the Sheridan and Gore Jones families.

The tug *Maud* (aquatint)

I had mentioned that she had connections with the Army, the Navy and the Church. The Navy we have dealt with. The Church was represented by her grandfather, Charlie, and her uncle Edmund James Satterthwaite, apart from other clergy descended from John Satterthwaite. The Army was represented by a number of the Phipps-Hornbys and her maternal great uncles, Colonel Joseph Henry Satterthwaite (died 1924 aged 85) and Colonel Benjamin Arthur Satterthwaite (died 1930 aged 81). As these officers add little to our story, other than perhaps to demonstrate the general longevity of the Satterthwaites, there is no need to mention them again.

Antecedents having been established, it is time to observe the widowed Mrs Satterthwaite and her four unmarried children at Stonehurst from 1916 onwards.

Chapter Eight

Life at Stonehurst – the first twenty years

We have been somewhat side-tracked in tracing and proving, in Lettie's words, that the Satterthwaites were well connected. As we have seen, they were. It is now time to join the twentieth-century Satterthwaites in Buxton.

The household at Stonehurst consisted initially of Mrs Satterthwaite and her three daughters, Maud, Lettie and Mary. The girls' brother Francis Edmund Sheridan Satterthwaite, known as Frank (born 1892), was not to join them until the end of the First World War in 1918, when he was released from Army duties.

All three girls were of marriageable age, and indeed Maud was 25 which in those days was considered to be getting rather old for marriage. The ranks of suitable men had been thinned by the First World War and, in any event, Mrs Satterthwaite did not encourage her daughters to marry.

Amongst the photo albums there are no pictures of any of the four Satterthwaite children at Dalton Hall, so whether or not they visited is not known. There is no reason why they should for the relationship between the Hornbys there and themselves was somewhat distant; it was their grandmother Victoria Susan Satterthwaite who died in 1906 (when Lettie was 11) who had been brought up there. Her brother (ie. their great uncle) died in 1923 with no children and the estate was inherited by a second cousin.

There were probably visits to London relatives, such as the Gore-Jones family, while the Satterthwaites lived at The Grange. With the move to Buxton all such visits probably ceased although there were a couple of the late Mr Satterthwaite's sisters living in the south. I never heard Lettie say that she had been to London after her arrival in Buxton.

LIFE AT STONEHURST – THE FIRST TWENTY YEARS

The move from Kenley to Buxton in 1916 must have been quite a shock. Instead of live-in staff, the family had to rely on a daily cook and other domestic staff that came in on a regular basis. So the coal fires, for instance, would not be started until someone had arrived to clean out the grates and get the fires going.

Breakfast might not be the sort of running buffet that they had been used to, members of the family appearing downstairs when it suited, as there was no longer live in staff. In any event, it could not now be served until the daily cook had arrived.

Whilst Mrs Satterthwaite was alive, it was understood that meals were served at set times and all the family had to eat together in the dining room. Lettie explained that each of them had an allotted place at the table and that each of them continued to occupy the same place even after their mother died. It saved argument. They never ate in the kitchen.

They did not of course need to go shopping for food; that was delivered. There was no motor car.

Because of their changed reduced circumstances, the family lived modestly. Although they had all the facilities to entertain well – a large dining room with a dining table sufficient to accommodate 14 diners and impressive quantities of silverware, china and glassware – they felt that they could not afford to do so. In any event in wartime there was no question of entertaining.

The best china and glass was now removed to a storeroom on the top floor of the house. It was clear at the time of Lettie's death in 1986 that it had not been touched for many years.

Geoffrey Satterthwaite ('Uncle Geoffie'), Mrs Satterthwaite's brother, used to walk the ten miles or so to Buxton from Disley. This would be a

Charles Geoffrey Satterthwaite (Uncle Geoffie)

Mrs Gertrude Mary Charlotte Satterthwaite in 1933 (Lettie's mother)

rather pleasant walk over the moorland of the Goyt Valley. He could always stay the night before returning, although he apparently rarely did so, preferring to walk back, especially if it was a summer's evening. Alternatively he could take the train as the Buxton to Manchester train called at Disley.

Otherwise there were probably few visitors and few excursions. For the first two years in Buxton there was a war on so travel would be difficult. All the grandparents were dead and there was therefore no 'required family visiting'. In any event, they needed to get settled in to their new life.

Lettie acquired a goat, whether out of necessity because of war shortages or out of curiosity is not known. Several photographs show her dealing with a goat in the outhouses of Stonehurst. There appears at one time to have been a donkey too.

Food shortages began to occur, and rationing of food was introduced in 1918. Ration cards were issued and everyone had to register with a local butcher and grocer. Sugar was rationed in January 1918. By the end of April, meat, butter, cheese and margarine were added to the list. Butter remained rationed until 1920. The Satterthwaites registered with the butcher's business of Mr Mycock and that business was still supplying Stonehurst with meat, butter and cheese, some 60 odd years later.

Mrs Satterthwaite, apparently oblivious to wartime difficulties, frequented the local sale rooms, purchasing the odd ornament to fill a display cabinet in the main drawing room at Stonehurst.

Maud seemed content to spend long hours in her room at the top of the house. She read her father's novels. She also compiled various family trees relying on books and family knowledge (there was no internet then!). These family trees did not solely relate to her own family; Edward IV (King of England 1461 to 1470 and from 1471 to 1483) seemed to be a particular fascination possibly because he was said to have been 6 feet 4 inches tall and both handsome and affable!

Maud must have spent hours putting together scrapbooks which showed crests of naval and military battalions, hotels and other institutions which sported a coat of arms. She also kept a very detailed account book showing how her savings increased.

Life in these early days in Buxton followed a pattern similar to that portrayed in the diaries of Victoria Susan Hornby some sixty years earlier, although less vivacious.

There were no domestic duties to be carried out. They had not been brought up to do those and had no inclination to do so. In any event they still managed to obtain domestic staff to deal with domestic chores. As far as Lettie and Mary were concerned, the days could be spent sewing and reading, researching dog pedigrees, writing letters and taking a daily walk. The walk to Solomon's Temple through Grin Low Woods was a great and regular favourite.

It is doubtful, even in later years, if any of the Satterthwaites (with the possible exception of Maud) had ever set foot in a supermarket or done any cooking, ironing, cleaning or washing up.

There must have been great excitement, but apprehension too, when Frank returned from the War in late 1918. He, of course, was returning to a household very different from the one he had left. His father had died in

Francis Edmund Sheridan Satterthwaite (Frank) at the onset of the First World War

1916, and the household was now in Buxton, not Kenley.

Frank was now 26, and unmarried. He had served as a sergeant in the Royal Army Medical Corp during the war, seeing service in France and Flanders and receiving the appropriate service medals.

He had left Eton College in December 1911 to 'go into business', according to college records. By his Will his father had left him a bequest of preference and ordinary shares in Tufnell Satterthwaite and Company Limited and one might therefore have expected that he might have joined his father's old firm of insurance underwriters. He might even have joined the Thames Steam Tug and Lighterage Co. Ltd where the family had connections. But it was not to be.

Frank was said to have been affected by gas in the First World War. Once he reached Buxton, he never did work and the only picture of him as an adult showed someone rather old and frail, compared with the strapping young man who had gone to war.

In a family as well connected as this, it was not unexpected that Frank should have been schooled at Eton. His father had been educated there and won a claret jug for the Old Boys' Quarter Mile in 1880. And, of course, James John Hornby (a Dalton Hall relative) had been headmaster there from 1868 to 1884. This might have been of some persuasive influence as to where Frank should be schooled.

Alas, Frank didn't show any academic or sporting success and the Eton College records confirm that 'no school sports, prizes or office positions' were attained. He did, however, play cricket and football for his house.

19th January 2017

Dear Mr Hartley,

Thank you for your recent enquiry regarding Francis E.S. Satterthwaite. Please find below his entry in the published school registers:

Satterthwaite (P.W., E.V.S.) — FRANCIS EDMUND SHERIDAN. Son of J. S. S. of Stonehurst, Buxton, Derbys.; 1906¹–1911³; served as 2nd Lieut. Loyal N. Lancs. Regt. in the War 1914–19. *Stonehurst, Buxton, Derbys.*

This shows that he arrived in the Summer Half 1906, and left in the Michaelmas Half 1911. He was in the house of Philip Williams, with Edward Vere Slater [EVS] as his tutor. No school sports, prizes or office positions are mentioned, suggesting he did not attain any. He did however play cricket and football (i.e. the field game) for his house. He left Eton in December 1911 to go into business, the exact nature of which is sadly not recorded.

With regards to records, we have the Head Master's Entrance Book, signed by all new boys on arrival; the School Clerk's Register, giving exact dates, prep school etc; and the Eton College Chronicle, the school magazine. This latter has been digitised and can be viewed online at http://archives.etoncollege.com

In addition, we have house books for PW, covering house sports events and the house debating society. We also have calendars which would give his exact timetable.

For more general information, the best source is the book by Tim Card, *Eton Renewed: A History from 1860 to the present day*, published by John Murray in 1994. This will give you an overview of the school at the period, and the daily lives of the boys.

You would be very welcome to come and use our Readers' Room to conduct your own research if you would like. We are open by appointment only, Monday to Friday, 9.30am – 1pm, 2pm – 4.45pm.

I'm afraid we are unable to offer a research service, so I am returning your cheque. In the meantime, I hope the above is of some interest.

Yours sincerely,

Eleanor Hoare (Mrs)
College Archivist

Eton College letter (2017)

Although Frank had been educated at Eton for the usual full five years, there is no evidence that any of his old Etonian chums came to stay at Stonehurst, even though Frank had three unmarried sisters. Perhaps this was discouraged by Mrs Satterthwaite who, as previously mentioned, had no desire to see them married.

It would appear that Frank, like Maud, was content to lead a quiet life at the top of the house indulging his interest in photography and as a radio ham, networking with others interested in communicating by radio.

One of the storerooms on the top floor was converted into a photographic darkroom for Frank. We are talking of a time well before the digital camera. Frank would have had all the chemical dishes and special lighting required to develop negatives and produce prints, a very time consuming procedure.

So far as radio was concerned, I remember seeing the various earphones, transmitters and batteries still at Stonehurst some twenty years after his death. Very little was ever thrown out! Indeed, after Frank's death there was apparently a scramble by the sisters to get hold of his handkerchieves. As Lettie, who was the victor, explained, 'men's handkerchieves are larger than those of ladies and are much more useful when one has a cold'.

But it was not perhaps as dull as an existence as it sounds. It was rumoured that at one time Frank courted May Langford, who lived with her parents in a large house on nearby Temple Road.

Janet May Langford was born in 1894, so was two years younger than Frank. In the 1911 Census her family was living in a 12-roomed house in Didsbury, a fashionable and expensive suburb of South Manchester. By the early 1920s the family was living in Buxton at Broomcroft, Temple Road, a substantial good looking house with a large garden. It still stands although now converted into two dwellings and, alas, looking somewhat neglected.

Mr Langford, May's father, was to die in late 1928, leaving an impressive estate of £82,592. Even in 1939, the Langford household could boast of two live-in servants, one of them a cook.

This would have been a very suitable match, but there was a defect. Mr Langford was engaged in trade as a skirt manufacturer in Manchester. The Satterthwaites were 'well connected'. A marriage with trade was not 'quite the thing' if one was so well connected. That Frank could not financially support a wife was probably a secondary consideration! The courtship came to nothing.

May Langford, who later became a JP in the town and never married, was as tall and outwardly as respectable as the Satterthwaites, It was always said that her erect figure owed much to her corsets.

She continued to live with her mother at Broomcroft until her mother died in 1956, aged 86. May herself died in 1984. If Frank had married her, no doubt the Satterthwaite story would have been very different!

One can imagine that living at home as a single man with no occupation, under the influence of a strong minded mother and three unmarried sisters, must have been a little difficult for Frank. It was hinted that he had a

Broomcroft, Temple Road, Buxton (2019), home of the Langford family, now two dwellings

partiality to alcohol, of which there would have been little at home. Resort to the bottle would certainly have been understandable. Apparently, Lettie and Mary came across him sleeping in the fields from time to time – alone!

Maud probably saw more of Frank than any other member of the family. They were of course closest in age and he would very often be on the top floor going to his darkroom or pursuing his radio interests. Her room was across the landing from these activities. No doubt he also called in on Maud to chat about her activities and to join with her in moaning about the other two sisters!

When Maud died, a trunk was discovered in her room. Lettie explained that Maud had envisaged leaving the household and setting up home with Frank. The trunk contained unused linens and other household items required for such purpose.

The real activity of the household however centred around Lettie and Mary and their dogs. As can be seen from the photograph, both of them were physically strong and imposing in their looks and height. They would certainly dominate the lesser Maud and the weaker Frank.

Lettie had been interested in dogs from an early age, and was never without one. She and Mary researched their pedigrees. They read dog lovers'

Lettie with two dogs outside Stonehurst (1927)

magazines. They were a common sight in the woods and fields opposite the house leading up to Soloman's Temple, dressed in their long brown coats and wearing their wide-brimmed brown felt hats, usually accompanied by several dogs.

Over the years they had Jerry, Rodger, Tony, Bonzo, Rob, Jet and Spot to name just a few of the dogs.

They did not stick to one particular breed of dog. Collies, Airedales, Spaniels and Labradors inhabited Stonehurst at one time or another. Lettie's Will was particular in bequeathing her 'pedigree charts relating to flat coated retrievers' to another dog lover.

Lettie and Mary occasionally attended dog shows, taking their own sandwiches with them as they did not trust other people's catering. They were well known to dog lovers in and around Buxton and, in earlier days, to dog breeders further afield.

They travelled by train to the odd dog show, sometimes venturing as far as Lytham St. Annes. But generally they stayed near to home. It was cheaper that way.

The photograph album shows that Lettie and Mary did have holidays. Their grandmother, Victoria Susan Satterthwaite, had travelled widely as her sketches show, even going abroad. It is doubtful if any of the Satterthwaite daughters travelled overseas. Indeed, there were no passports among their respective papers.

The years 1930 to 1934 saw a number of holidays. One of these – almost certainly a coach tour – saw them over a period of 17 days in 1930 visit Ludlow, Ross on Wye, Glastonbury, Tavistock, Fowey, Bridgwater, Broadway, Stratford, Kenilworth and Lichfield.

The following year saw a visit to Wales and the Conway Valley. Thereafter, Lettie and Mary seemed to limit their visits to West Kirby, Southport and Lytham St. Annes. This was probably because they could take the dogs with them. There is no evidence that their mother, Maud or Frank went with them.

Somehow or another, the household carried on without much change during the difficult 1920s, the General Strike of 1926, the political upheavals of the politics of the early 1930s and the deflationary pressures of the years before the Second World War.

They did not appear to involve themselves in committee or charitable work. There is no evidence of any interest in politics. Reading the Daily Telegraph seemed to keep them sufficiently informed. They seemed content to lead a rather undemanding life.

During the 1930s, the then Headmaster of Buxton College, which was within a quarter of a mile distant from Stonehurst, accepted about 30 refugee boys of Jewish extraction as boarders. This apparently met with a fair amount of local criticism. The boys would have been seen on and around Green Lane.

The fact that I never heard about any of this from Lettie, even though it must have been a local cause célèbre, reinforced my view that generally she was a tolerant and fair minded woman.

The year of 1935 however saw family sadness and disappointment with the death of Uncle Geoffie. We should perhaps devote a little time to him before continuing the story of life at Stonehurst.

Chapter Nine

Uncles, Aunts and Uncle Geoffie – a surprising disappointment

Considering the number of children in earlier generations, the number of uncles and aunts of the four Satterthwaites in Buxton was relatively modest. Their father had been one of five children who survived infancy, whilst their mother was one of three.

On their father's side, two aunts survived into the 1950s, but there appears to have been only one cousin and she died without children in 1963. I never heard mention of any of these relatives and so have no idea where they lived or how they were placed in the world. I think I would have heard if they had achieved distinction as that would be another good connection!

Their mother had two younger brothers, Edmund and Geoffrey, known within the family respectively as Eddie and Geoffie.

Edmund had been educated at Charterhouse School and Jesus College, Cambridge (his father's old college) and was ordained in 1891, going first as a curate to Epping, then returning to Disley where he was curate to his father's parish from 1892 to 1898. This would have been a comfortable post with his parents still living at The Parsonage. He too would have enjoyed the services of their domestic staff.

By 1898, with his marriage scheduled for the following year, he was Vicar of Broad Chalke, near Salisbury. The living was in the gift of Kings College, Cambridge and no doubt his own education and his father's position as a Canon of Chester Cathedral and long standing Vicar of Disley helped to secure the appointment.

It would appear to have been a decent parish to secure, endowed with a handsome house as the watercolour by his mother shows.

His marriage to Adelaide Wynne Pennant of Nantlys, Flintshire, did not result in any children. The couple left the parish in 1908, moving

All Saints' Church, Broad Chalke, near Salisbury, a watercolour by VSS (1899)

Broad Chalke Vicarage, a watercolour by VSS (1899)

Adelaide Wynne Pennant (later Mrs Edmund James Satterthwaite)

to Eastbourne where Edmund acted as a curate of All Saints' Church until his death in 1922, aged 56.

He is commemorated at Broad Chalke by his wife paying for the restoration of the church tower and windows in 1924/25.

Adelaide Satterthwaite, aged 51 at the time of her husband's death, returned to North Wales, dying in a St. Asaph nursing home in October 1960, aged 89. She left a goodly estate of £31,672, which would have come in very useful had it been left to her late husband's nieces in Buxton. But it went elsewhere.

Uncle Geoffie's life, in contrast, appears to have been much more interesting than that of his elder brother, who was seven years his senior.

We have seen that Uncle Geoffie used to come over to Buxton from Disley to visit the household at Stonehurst, sometimes staying the night before getting the train back to Disley.

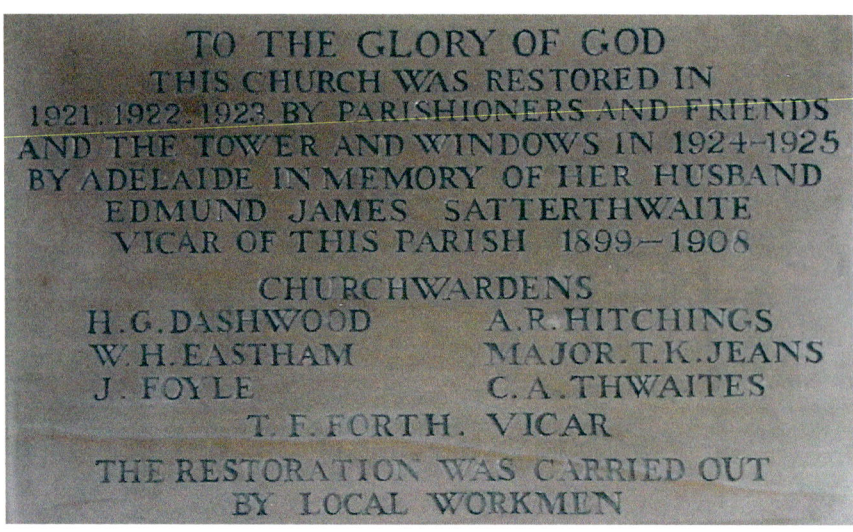

Restoration plaque at Broad Chalke Church

Uncle Geoffie as a boy,
Disley Parsonage,
a watercolour by VSS

He brightened up the household and was a great favourite with the girls. Lettie was his godchild. She recalled that when Uncle Geoffie came to stay the best dinner service was produced and that there was brandy and champagne. There must have been quite an upheaval as the best china would have to be brought down from the upstairs storeroom, but no doubt it was worth it for the liveliness that Uncle Geoffie's visit provided.

Getting out the best china would no doubt allow the family to speculate on the meaning behind the raised sword dripping with drops of blood which was emblazoned on the china. This was apparently the Satterthwaite crest but I never did find out to what the emblem referred.

Charles Geoffrey Satterthwaite was born at Disley Parsonage and remained there until his father died in June 1910, at which time he was 37 years of age.

A Satterthwaite plate with the emblem of a raised sword dripping with blood.

Like most men of his time, he couldn't cook or look after himself. Life at the parsonage had been very comfortable with domestic staff and a cook. But now he had to leave the parsonage as it was required for his father's successor, Rev. Harold Haworth, who was to remain in post until 1924.

What better than to move to The Ram's Head in Disley, and that is where Uncle Geoffie was listed as living at the time of the April 1911 Census.

The Ram's Head was a convenient location. It is next to the railway station, so convenient for Uncle Geoffie's occupation as an Assistant Travel Manager for the Great Central Railway. It was also not far from Disley Golf Club where he had been a member for over 10 years.

The duties of an Assistant Travel Manager appear rather vague. All one can surmise is that such duties did not require a great deal of hard work – they certainly did not appear to impede upon games of golf or trips to Buxton! One's understanding of Uncle Geoffie is that he liked to enjoy life.

On the death of Rev. Satterthwaite in 1910, the various Hornby trusts from which his wife Victoria Susan had enjoyed the income (and which the Rev. Satterthwaite enjoyed during his further lifetime) came to an end.

The trust funds passed equally to the three Disley Parsonage children – Gertrude (Mrs Satterthwaite), Edmund and Geoffie. In addition Geoffie inherited the whole of his father's estate after legacies of £5,000 to Edmund and £500 to Gertrude, and so received about £44,000. This, together with the trust monies received, would certainly have enabled him to live at The Ram's Head.

Rev. Satterthwaite's Will seems rather inequitable as one might have expected him to have treated his children equally. Possibly he felt that Gertrude

Cross Hill, Torrisholme, near Morecambe

Uncle Geoffie at Cross Hill

was already well set up (her husband was still alive) and Edmund appears to have got himself settled into a pretty comfortable Living. He probably thought that Geoffie as a single man would need additional monies if he was to have a household of his own.

It is not known when Geoffie left Disley. He possibly waited until his sister Gertrude was well settled in Buxton. He was now a wealthy man and single. He certainly had no need to work.

His father had left him interests in properties at Overton and Bazil, together with interests in properties in Lancaster. His parents were both buried at Overton and he had an unmarried uncle at Dalton Hall. It might have been in his mind, no more, that Uncle Edmund Geoffrey Stanley Hornby could possibly leave him the Dalton Hall estate. That was not to be when the uncle died in 1923.

A change of area, where he was not as well known as he would be in Disley, might also allow him to 'spread his wings'. All in all, it was not unexpected that he should be drawn back to Lancaster.

Uncle Geoffie purchased a decent sized house known as Cross Hill, Torrisholme, near Morecambe, about three miles from Overton and nine miles from Dalton Hall. He also purchased a nearby cottage, presumably to house a member of staff.

With this new way of life he must have decided to have a bit of fun. He ran a couple of motor cars, he met up with his unmarried cousin, Charles Windham Leycester Penrhyn-Hornby who had inherited Dalton Hall, and he acquired a lady friend.

It was the emergence of the lady friend that was to cause disappointment.

In the 1930s life was beginning to be a little difficult at Stonehurst; staff were harder to obtain and money did not seem to go as far as previously. Her brother became ill but Gertrude would have been confident that he would 'do the decent thing' and leave his estate to his only nephew and nieces, her four children.

It was quite a surprise and a considerable disappointment therefore when Uncle Geoffie died aged only 62 on 9 June 1935, leaving his cars, his house and nearby cottage and £25,000 to his 'friend Aileen Beatrice Clifford Ruddy'. She was also to have the use of his furniture during her lifetime, these chattels to pass to his sister Gertrude on her decease.

The original Will made in January 1932 had only left Aileen Ruddy £20,000 and the use of Uncle Geoffie's house and cottage for her life. On her death the income from the proceeds of these properties would have gone to Gertrude for her life with the capital going to her four children on her death. This is as one might have expected.

But, by April 1934 Uncle Geoffie had a change of heart. Aileen Ruddy's potential inheritance was substantially upgraded. Aileen was to get his house and cottage outright and the increased sum of £25,000. The remainder of his estate was to pass to Gertrude's children.

The total estate was £82,000 from which death duties of £16,500 were paid. After payment of the legacy to Aileen, and some other legacies to staff, there was probably just under £40,000 left from which the value of the house and cottage were to be deducted. The balance between Gertrude's four children would have amounted to something in the order of £8,000 each – quite a decent amount but a considerable disappointment compared with the expectation.

One suspects that the inhabitants of Stonehurst did not know much about Aileen Ruddy so the *Lancaster Evening Post* of 14 September 1935 giving details of the terms of the Will with the headline '£25,000 left to a friend', apart from their disappointment, would have rather rubbed salt in the wound.

And then, of course, there was the suggestion implied by the headline, that Aileen had been more than just a friend. Respectability was still important. After all, Geoffie was the son of a well respected clergyman who might have been remembered in Lancaster circles.

Uncle Geoffie in 1934 with nurse

Some respectability however was maintained as Aileen's address in the Will was given as 'care of' her sister Mrs Broadbent of Pendleton, Manchester. Their father had been an Insurance Superintendent with the Prudential Assurance Company.

A closer relationship than just a friend was perhaps confirmed by Aileen's own probate some 16 years later in 1951.

When a deceased is known by more than one name, it is customary to apply for a grant of probate to his or her estate in the legal name of the deceased and the assumed name. This saves a lot of trouble in collecting in the assets which might be registered in either name.

The probate to Aileen Ruddy's estate was issued in the name of 'Aileen Beatrice Clifford Ruddy or Satterthwaite'. Although she was there described as a Spinster, the reader is left to draw their own conclusion.

In the event, she died on 12 March 1951 at The Pier Hotel, Dun Laoghaire, Kingstown, Ireland but having an address at South Shore, Blackpool. She was 77. Her estate amounted to £9,775 suggesting that quite a lot of Uncle Geoffie's largesse had been spent!

There was perhaps one happy outcome from Uncle Geoffie's death. It is thought that he had been nursed in his last illness by Cicely Mary Townley. She was descended from Elizabeth Satterthwaite, a daughter of John Satterthwaite. So although Cicely was a great, great, great grandchild of John Satterthwaite and Geoffie was only a great grandchild of John Satterthwaite, they were related.

It is thought that Lettie met Cicely when visiting Uncle Geoffie. They were to become good friends.

Uncle Geoffie was buried at Overton Church.

£25,000 LEFT TO A FRIEND

Torrisholme Retired Official's Will

£87,000 ESTATE

MR. CHARLES GEOFFREY SATTERTHWAITE, of Cross Hill, Torrisholme, near Morecambe, retired railway official, who died on June 9th last, aged 62, son of the late Canon Satterthwaite, left estate of the gross value of £87,938 1s. 4d., with net personalty £82,408 2s. 6d.

Probate of his will, with three codicils, has been granted to his cousin, Charles Windham Leycester Penrhyn-Hornby, of Dalton Hall, Burton, Westmorland, and Hubert Lister Farrar solicitor, of 79, Fountain-street, Manchester.

Newspaper Headline 1935

Chapter Ten

Continuing life at Stonehurst – the separate lives of Maud and Lettie

It seems clear that come the late 1930s the household at Stonehurst was struggling economically to survive. There had been a little boost to the occupants' fortunes from Uncle Geoffie's death. Further funds might come on the death of Uncle Edmund's widow (although that was not to be) and maybe some inheritance might yet come from their father's surviving unmarried sister. As there had been little contact, that was unlikely (as proved to be the case).

There had been little contact with these relatives because the household was struggling to survive and constant economy was required.

Nothing had been done to the house for twenty years. It was proving more difficult to get staff and prices seemed to be rising. Fortunately the sisters showed no interest in clothes. They managed with what they had.

Lettie and Mary became more involved with their dogs and Maud and Frank more to their own quarters and interests. By the start of World War Two in 1939 Mrs Satterthwaite was in her late 70s. She continued to rule the household but increasingly withdrew to her own capacious bedroom on the first floor with its magnificent views over Temple Fields and beyond. Here she could muse on her childhood visits to Dalton Hall, her well connected family and her married life of 26 years. She probably read some of her late husband's books housed in the bookcase in the dining room, but there is little evidence that she was a great reader.

Mary took over some of the household tasks such as paying the gardener and the household bills. She organised the cooking (she didn't of course cook herself) and the running of the house.

It was probably about this time that the drawing room ceased to be used as such. Lettie and Mary, whilst leaving its furniture in situ, took it

Mary with two dogs at Stonehurst

over as a depository for their dog magazines and as a haven for any dog that they were nursing.

By all accounts throughout the Second World War, they scoured the local farms for meat for their own dogs and dogs of others. If a sheep died, the Misses Satterthwaite soon got to hear of it and were there to claim the carcass, notwithstanding any regulations.

It was well known among dog lovers of Buxton that a needy dog would not be turned away from Stonehurst.

Somehow the household survived the shortages of war, the bitter winter of 1947, the coal strike and what was regarded by them as ruinous and penal taxation. The post war Labour Government had no supporters at Stonehurst.

Mrs Satterthwaite died in January 1954, aged 92, having been a widow for 38 years. She left £30,151, still a decent sum of money when a detached house could be purchased for £2,000, but not a lot when divided by four and when there was a big house to run. Her death also brought to an end the trust established by her late husband's will from which she had received the income. This fund was distributed between the four children. One suspects that this fund had not grown much in value since their father's death.

Frank died the following year aged 63. He left no will. As might be expected, Maud dealt with his estate, which was divided equally between the three sisters, according to the rules relating to an intestacy. His estate, which included what he had inherited from his mother and his father's estate, amounted to £15,629.

A burial plot large enough to accommodate five had been purchased at Christ Church, Burbage, on the outskirts of Buxton. It is there that all five members of the family are interred. Cremation had not been permitted in England until 1884 but the Satterthwaites were of the old school and burial was preferred.

Fortunately, Lettie had told me about the grave and that it had been configured to hold three on one side and two on the other. When she died the undertakers told me that there was no room for her. They had only looked on one side! They were sent back, and Lettie was able to join her mother and Mary as she had intended.

Mrs Satterthwaite's burying was not without a little macabre drama. The Victorians, of whom of course she was one having been born in 1861, were terrified of being buried alive. Old legal books are full of precedents to be incorporated in a Will directing steps to be taken to ascertain that death had actually occurred before burial could take place. Many of us will be familiar with the notion of the bell on the top of a coffin attached to the deceased's toe, so that the bell would ring if the person to be buried was still alive.

In Mrs Satterthwaite's case, her corpse was placed in a coffin which rested on the dining table at Stonehurst. Only when, in Lettie's words, 'the body began to turn' would the family authorise the burial to be arranged.

When Maud died, Lettie canvassed the suggestion that Maud should similarly lie on the dining room table. Both Dr Willis and I managed to persuade her that such steps were outmoded, and that Maud was truly dead.

With Mrs Satterthwaite and Frank dead, the two Disley Uncles having died before the Second World War, and all the grandparents long since departed, the three sisters were left somewhat alone at Stonehurst.

Assuming that his sisters had roughly the same amount as Frank at the time of his death, this suggested that between them the three sisters had approximately £60,000. This would include the value of the house.

Whilst this could be considered a reasonable amount in the 1950s, with the rapid inflation that subsequently occurred the income produced was hardly going to be sufficient to keep a large house and its staff going. This was at a time when unearned income, such as that received from their investments, was taxed at a greater rate than earned income.

A regular visitor was Cicely Craven (cousin Cicely). She used to come to stay for several days at a time. I always felt that, other than in a warm summer, she must have been bitterly cold throughout her stay. She was put up in a rather inhospitable bedroom on the top floor of the house with little heating, little carpeting (just a square of carpet surrounded by linoleum) and thin unlined curtains, sleeping in a very old fashioned bed which looked most uncomfortable. On the plus side she would have had splendid views towards Grin Low Woods and Solomon's Temple.

The bathroom was on the floor below but she would have been provided with a wash bowl and ewer of water.

Another visitor, but not to stay, was Diana Lawrence, the youngest daughter of Sir Ernest Wingate Saul, KC. She used to visit with her cousin, Pamela Johnson, motoring over from Sheffield. Both these ladies were related to the Satterthwaites, Mrs Lawrence as her mother was a Satterthwaite and Mrs Johnson as her father was a Satterthwaite. These were both children of Thomas Edmundson Satterthwaite, a brother to Rev. Charlie and a son of James Cornelius.

Mrs Lawrence recalled a rather desultory lunch in the large dining room at Stonehurst. A maid served and a bell was rung for the table to be cleared when they had finished their meal. She commented that the food was completely unmemorable.

Conversation at lunch apparently centred round the probable cost of replacing the brown linoleum in the long hall and the iniquity of the high level of super tax. Mrs Lawrence, when she left, couldn't decide if her relatives were very rich, and miserly, or very poor. Certainly, after paying staff, there would have been little to spare out of their income.

As the daughters had inherited equally on their mother's death, it was agreed that each would pay one third of the expenses of running the house.

Lettie and Mary continued to use the front sitting room. The large drawing room was by now completely abandoned and given over to storage. Maud continued to live in relative isolation in her large bed-sitting room on the top floor.

Discord arose from the fact that Maud's room was heated by electricity, whilst the downstairs sitting room was heated by a coal fire, and occupied by the two other sisters. It was felt by them that Maud benefitted disproportionately. The end result was the fitting of a separate electricity meter which recorded the exact usage of Maud's electricity, which she now had to pay for separately. Similarly, consumption of milk was disputed. A separate book was therefore kept with consumption being recorded and the bill being apportioned accordingly.

Lettie and Mary were close and did everything together. They found Maud difficult, not helped by her deafness. Maud and her brother Frank

Lettie at Lytham with her dog

had been close and had contemplated setting up house together. So, after Frank's death Maud was somewhat in limbo.

She may at one time have harboured thoughts of marriage for, in the trunk that she kept filled with domestic essentials if she and Frank had left home, she kept a book entitled 'What every woman should know about her body'.

Maud was a little inquisitive. She would hunt information down that interested her. Her two younger sisters were content to spend their time concerned about the dogs. They pooh-poohed Maud's investigations and interests.

Poor Maud, apart from being a little deaf, became much shorter and smaller than her two much more dominant sisters. It was not surprising that she retreated into her shell. Relations became such that Maud ate alone in the dining room at her allotted place and only after she had finished and taken her plates to the kitchen did the other two sisters come in to sit down to eat.

After Mary's death, this separation continued with Lettie and Maud eating separately at different times. Standards were not relaxed; they sat in the cavernous dining room to eat. There was no eating in the kitchen even though it might have been warmer and certainly more convenient for the daily cook.

It was not long after my introduction to the Satterthwaites that Lettie gave me a conducted tour of the house. I saw the kitchen, the pantries, the back stairs, the storerooms, Frank's dark room and radio shack, Mrs

Satterthwaite's room and everywhere else. Lettie had told me to keep my coat on and I was glad I had done so. The coal fires in the hall and Lettie's sitting room were hardly sufficient to keep the house warm.

Lettie explained that to keep the chill at bay there was an electric heater on the landing, which was only unplugged at night. She was worried about the cost of using this heater; the electric plug apparently got so hot that she had to use a wet tea towel in order to unplug it!

On enquiry it seemed that apart from fitting the extra electricity meter to control Maud's 'extravagance', and some dubious wiring fitted by Frank, no electrical work had been carried out in the house since they took occupation in 1916, nearly 60 years earlier.

I persuaded Lettie that Mr Soper, a long standing electrician in Buxton, should call. He convinced Lettie that the house should be rewired! In spite of the expense Lettie quickly agreed to the rewiring and once the risk of electrocution by using the wet tea towel had been explained to Maud, she willingly agreed to pay half the cost.

Maud did not appear to bear any grudge against her sisters and was obviously anxious to see that her affairs were in order and to do 'the decent thing'. Without appointment, on a very wet day, she arrived clad in her dripping pacamac, at my office. She had hunted me out. She wished to make a Will leaving her estate to Lettie. She instructed that any letters to be sent to her were to be in plain envelopes and not to pass through our office franking machine. She feared trouble if Lettie, who commandeered the post on arrival, knew that she was in contact with a solicitor.

In the event, when I arrived at Stonehurst one day to see Lettie, she said to me, 'you have been writing to Maud'. She knew I had for she had seen the envelopes with a typewritten address and recognised the size of the envelope. Fortunately, before I needed to reply, Maud appeared. She told Lettie that she was making her Will. Nothing further was said and no question as to the contents of Maud's Will were asked of me.

Maud did do 'the decent thing'. In her Will dated 4 April 1978 she left all her estate to Lettie, dying before her on 25 February 1982. Before her death however there was an incident of some note at Stonehurst.

CHAPTER ELEVEN

The Fire

It was a dark cold September night in 1981. Lettie was in her sitting room on the ground floor of Stonehurst enjoying the warmth of a good coal fire with her dog at her side. The fire in the hall had been allowed to die down. The electric heater on the landing was on its usual low setting, just enough to take the Buxton chill out of the air. Following the recent re-wiring this was no longer the fire hazard it once was.

Maud, now 91, had shuffled down the staircase to make a hot milk drink in the kitchen before going upstairs to bed. Her room was cold and her bed inhospitable. She decided that by holding her small electric fire over the bed, she would have a warm bed to get into. The idea of the purchase of an electric blanket was an extravagance that had not been thought of!

Unfortunately, she was unable to hold the fire firmly above the bed. She dropped it onto the bed. Before she could cross the room to unplug the fire, the bed was alight. Smoke billowed.

Lettie must have sensed or heard that something was amiss. Perhaps her dog alerted her.

She came out of her room and shouted up the staircase to Maud, 'what are you doing'. Receiving no reply she mounted the stairs, but then saw the smoke. Going as quickly as she could – she was 87 at the time – she descended the stairs and crossed the hall. She unlocked the dining room door and hastened to the far end of the room where the telephone was in a locked cabinet, so secured so as to thwart unauthorised use.

The telephone being released she dialled 999. She was asked if she wanted 'Police, Fire or Ambulance'. Her response was unhesitating – 'you'd better send the lot'. Asked for her address, she replied 'Stonehurst, Green Lane', and then put the 'phone down.

In what must have seemed like an age, she waited for the emergency services to arrive. She could hear the clanging of the fire engine's bell and the wail of sirens, but no vehicles appeared. Of course, if she had given her address as 'number 32 Green Lane' instead of 'Stonehurst' that would have made life easier for the emergency services! However, her wits did not desert her. She got hold of a large hand bell which was kept at the front door for such emergencies and stood at the garden gate ringing it for all she was worth.

All the services arrived and were directed to the top of the house, the firemen unreeling their hoses as they ran in. Smoke was now billowing down the staircase. Lettie told them that Maud was on the top floor.

A young fireman ran up the two flights of stairs and stumbled over what he thought was a sack of rubbish. An anguished cry revealed that it was Maud. Realising his mistake, the fireman hoisted Maud up in a fireman's lift and popped her over his shoulder. This was too much.

Frightened, but outraged at being so manhandled, Maud kicked her little shoes against the poor fireman. He was very much bruised and reportedly off work the next day with a badly bruised rib cage.

The fire was extinguished. Maud was taken to the Buxton Cottage Hospital and Lettie telephoned me the next day. I was asked to call to view

Maud's room at Stonehurst – left hand turret (2019)

the damage and details of the fire were related. I was asked what should be done. Fortunately the property and its contents were insured.

In the event, the damage was not as bad as all that. Obviously Maud's horsehair mattress was destroyed and the charred floorboards under her bed had to be replaced. A box of silverware stored under the bed for safekeeping had to be sent off for professional cleaning. Otherwise, thanks to the fire brigade, the fire had been quickly contained. The insurers paid out without undue difficulty. Surprisingly, there was little smoke damage. But what about Maud?

A visit to the Cottage Hospital showed Maud to be in high spirits. She had always had a twinkle in her eye. The strange surroundings did not seem to faze her. If anything she seemed to be stimulated by the activity around her. She was warm, clean and comfortable and well fed. Indeed, she was rather enjoying herself. There was plenty going on and, except for the indignity of being picked up and thrown over the shoulder of a young man, she was unharmed. Her concern, and that of Lettie, was for her future.

Lettie felt that she could not cope with Maud. The responsibility would be too great. For her part, Maud recognised that a return to Stonehurst would be difficult. In any case, having seen the activity around her, she rather fancied living somewhere brighter, warmer and cheerful – what about a private hotel?

After discussion, Maud moved to the Lismore Nursing Home where she seemed content. Lettie visited her from time to time as did fellow parishioners from St. Mary's Church.

Maud was 92 when she died in February 1982. Lettie was now alone at Stonehurst. But first, there was Maud's funeral.

Chapter Twelve

Maud's Funeral

Mr Percival was instructed to deal with Maud's funeral. Mr Percival had been an undertaker for a very long time. He looked like a character from one of Dickens' novels – thin, pale faced, lugubrious and cadaverous. One was always surprised to see him at a funeral for one had expected that he would have joined his clients long since.

Mr Percival had dealt with Mrs Satterthwaite's funeral in 1954 and that of Frank the following year. His black motor cars, well polished, were doubtless as old as he was.

There was to be a funeral service at St. Mary's Church, Dale Road, Buxton, where Maud had been a regular attender, followed by interment in the family grave at Christ Church, Burbage.

It had always been a puzzle to me as to why the Satterthwaite grave was at Christ Chrurch, Burbage whilst Maud had worshipped at St. Mary's Church, the full name of which is St. Mary the Virgin.

Research into the history of St. Mary's Church provided some of the answer. The foundation stone for St. Mary's was laid by Evelyn, Duchess of Devonshire on 26th May 1915 and the building was not completed until 1917. It is now a Grade II listed building as it was built in the style of the Arts and Crafts movement. It is perhaps remarkable that it was built in the First World War when manpower was heavily engaged elsewhere.

When the Satterthwaites moved to Buxton in 1916, St. Mary's did not exist. And, it does not have a graveyard. The big town church was, as now, the church of St. John the Baptist on St. John's Road, Buxton. This is a grand church of regency architecture and was built in 1811 following financial benefaction of the 5th Duke of Devonshire. It has been described as 'more like a small cathedral rather than a local church'. With its grand appearance and stained glass windows designed by the famous C. E. Kempe this would not have suited the low profile of the Satterthwaites. In any event, attendance would have required a goodly walk from Stonehurst.

Ignoring the little church of St. Anne's on Bath Road – very small, very old and with no graveyard space – this left Christ Church, Burbage. Built in 1861 it has a large graveyard and a striking south window by Morris & Co. designed by Burne-Jones. Whilst a good mile walk from Stonehurst it had a long serving vicar and would satisfy the family's requirements. Later years of course made St Mary's much more attractive for their worship and thus the service for Maud at St Mary's with a burial at Burbage.

Mrs Lawrence from Sheffield attended the funeral but did not make herself known, nor did she go to Stonehurst. Lettie must have spoken to her to inform her of Maud's death.

Lettie was ill, the nature of her illness unascertained. She may well have felt that to stand at a graveside on a bitterly cold February Buxton day might hasten her own death. She made it clear she could not attend the funeral. And so, it was Cicely Craven and myself who were the only persons in the funeral car which left Stonehurst for St. Mary's Church.

The church service was dignified. Possibly no more than 12 people were present. Mrs Craven and I then got into the funeral car to follow the hearse the two miles or so to Burbage.

Half way there, at Wye Head, opposite the bus stop, the hearse came to a halt. Our driver was instructed by the driver of the hearse to move our car forward so as to be in front of the hearse. This was all very strange.

At this point a bus arrived at the Stop on the other side of the road. The passengers and ourselves, for we could not resist turning round to watch what was going on, were treated to the sight of the tailgate of the hearse

St Mary's Church, Dale Road, Buxton (2019)

being raised to enable the driver to get at a can of petrol from the space underneath the coffin so that he could re-fuel his vehicle. We were told afterwards that the petrol gauge had long ceased to function! Mr Percival had hoped that there would be enough fuel in the tank to get us to Burbage.

Our car had been moved forward so that we should not be treated to the undignified sight of petrol cans and other paraphernalia stored in the back of the hearse.

I like to think that Maud would have enjoyed this bizarre spectacle. She was fond of a joke and had a great sense of humour. What the passengers on the bus made of it all, one can but speculate.

Anyway, refuelling complete, we were able to proceed to Burbage where Maud was properly buried.

Mrs Craven and I were then returned to Stonehurst. Lettie made a brief and dramatic appearance. She was dressed in a long, white flannel nightgown, which flowed down to her ankles. On top of this was the inevitable brown cardigan. Her hair was not in its usual bun, but was hanging loose. One's thoughts certainly turned to Miss Havisham as portrayed in Charles Dickens' *Great Expectations*. We were offered a cup of tea and some biscuits.

Lettie's appearance was to enquire about the events of the day. When told, she was not amused. She was glad it was all over.

Maud incidentally had been a careful saver and husbanded her resources well. Her estate was sworn at £114,000, a very creditable sum, and all of which went to Lettie. Her account books showed the credit balance carried forward each year and how her savings had multiplied. She had been a cautious investor with most of her savings held in Government Stocks. There were some premium savings bonds as well to provide a little excitement!

Unlike her late sister Mary's room, Maud's room was neat and tidy. She had few personal possessions. There were no dog magazines here.

Amongst her personal effects however was a small sealed tin. Lettie seemed to know about this. It apparently contained a portion of fruit cake made for Maud's christening. When the tin was opened, the cake looked perfectly good to me – I suppose it had been liberally laced with spirit – but Lettie insisted that it be thrown away. I often muse that a modern day nutritionist might have found it quite interesting to analyse a fruit cake over 90 years old.

Satterthwaite grave, Christ Church, Burbage, Buxton (July 2013)

Chapter Thirteen

Lettie alone, the trip to Lichfield and an unseemly outrage

Lettie was now alone at Stonehurst with her recently acquired dog, Paula, as her only company. There was still a daily cook, who carried out a few housekeeping tasks, but this must have been a difficult job. No tinned food or frozen foods were allowed and so far as dusting of furniture was concerned, this was almost impossible as all surfaces were covered by newspapers, dog magazines or pedigree charts.

Mrs Satterthwaite's room, Frank's room, Mary's room and now Maud's room were simply abandoned. The large drawing room had long since been given over to storage. So, apart from the kitchen area and bathroom, only Lettie's sitting room, her bedroom above, the hall and the dining room, were in daily use.

A local lad called in to wind the clocks, a man still came to tend the fires in Lettie's sitting room, the hall and the kitchen and an old retainer kept the garden to rights. The daily cook ordered the delivery of food, or collected it on her way to work.

Lettie continually worried as to whether or not she had enough money to continue to run the house, and worried also as to how she should deal with its contents.

Amongst the many possessions at Stonehurst was the so called Johnson Dictionary, being a dictionary compiled by Dr Samuel Johnson (1709–84) and given to Thomas Sheridan in 1755, its year of publication. It will be recalled (see Chapter seven) that a granddaughter, Frances Anna Georgiana Sheridan, had married Charles Satterthwaite and thus the descent of the dictionary to the Satterthwaite family.

Thomas Sheridan (1719–88), once he had returned to England from Ireland, established himself as a teacher and educator particularly with regard to elocution. In Bath he founded an Academy for the regular instruction of young gentlemen in the art of reading and grammatical knowledge of the English tongue.

In addition he published his own General Dictionary of the English Language, in 1780. As such, it is not surprising that he would know Dr Johnson and would have been given a copy of his dictionary.

It took Dr Johnson around nine years to compile the 42,000 definitions in the dictionary and the dictionary is contained in two hefty volumes. It was printed in London for a consortium of booksellers, including T. and T. Longman.

Lettie felt that the dictionary should be properly appreciated. She was fearful that if it was sold after her death, it would be purchased 'by the Americans'. After all it was a first edition and its provenance was unquestionable. She was clear that the dictionary should remain in the UK. The fact that it might be valuable and that a sale before her death might alleviate her financial worries was immaterial; the dictionary should stay in the UK and be exhibited in an appropriate place. Without question that was Lichfield, the place of Dr Johnson's birth.

Arrangements were accordingly made for the dictionary to go to the Samuel Johnson Birthplace Museum in Lichfield. She asked if I would take her. And Paula was to come too. The date was fixed for 1 July 1982.

Lichfield can't have seen anything like our arrival for a long time. There we were walking down the pedestrianised street, Paula on the end of a long piece of string followed by an 88 year old woman wearing a long brown coat down

Lettie with dogs in her field

Presentation of the Johnson Dictionary, *Lichfield Mercury*, 9 July 1982

to her ankles, a large brown wide brimmed felt hat trimmed with a white stripe, using a cane with a silver knob, and her stature and her demeanour marking her out as someone of note. I stumbled behind with the two volume leather bound dictionary which was very heavy.

The Museum did things properly. The Curator and the Mayor of Lichfield were present, photographs were taken and a cup of tea offered (but politely refused). Paula behaved impeccably.

There had been a slight flutter of anxiety on arrival. The signs were clear. No dogs other than guide dogs were to be allowed into the Museum. The lady on reception was about to enforce the Rule. Fortunately she had been briefed as to the purpose of our proposed visit. It was quite clear from Lettie's demeanour – no dog, no dictionary! Admission was granted.

The curator produced a family tree attached to an 1886 book on the Lives of the Sheridans by Percy Fitzgerald. Lettie was able to give some insight on some of the names; she had either met the people concerned or knew of them from her mother. This particularly applied to the Gore Jones connection. We were all very impressed as her reminiscences sounded so fresh.

The Curator said that the dictionary was probably the most important contribution to the displays since he had been working at the museum and he knew of no other first editions in the country. This was very pleasing and altogether it was a very satisfactory day.

Having dealt with the Dictionary, Lettie started to turn her mind to the other contents of Stonehurst. Such thoughts were interrupted by what Lettie considered to be an outrage against her property.

The two fields opposite Stonehurst, and owned by her, had been allowed to go wild. They however provided a convenient place to walk the dog as increasing age made walks to Solomon's Temple and elsewhere physically difficult.

Derbyshire County Council, who owned the land on the other side of the fields, decided to construct a playing field. In so doing they not only trespassed on to Lettie's land but purported to take part of it by putting up a rather flimsy fence on what they considered to be the appropriate boundary. This fence was much inferior to the stone wall they had removed.

A telephoned complaint by Lettie to the Council was dealt with dismissively. Officers were too busy to see to what, by all accounts, was a trifling matter troubling an old lady. I was called in to write to the Council.

At the age of nearly 90, Lettie found herself likely to be the Plaintiff in proceedings against a County Council, if they did not put things right. This was unfortunate but property rights were to be respected. It was made clear to the County Council that Lettie was not to be fobbed off.

Fortunately the threat of proceedings brought officials to their senses. An official of proper status – not just 'a chit of a girl' – came to apologise, a boundary was agreed, the County Council paid for the appropriate stone walling and by November 1982 a deed between the parties confirmed the agreed position of the boundary.

This was a satisfactory outcome but had not been achieved without anxiety. Once agreement had been reached, Lettie enjoyed the activity of a twice daily inspection with Paula to make sure that the wall was built to a proper standard.

In the summer of 1983 Lettie's doctor advised that she should no longer live alone. She was told that someone should live in the house 24 hours a day. This was fine for the daytime as Mrs Norton was coming in daily as a cook/housekeeper.

To everyone's surprise Lettie was quite amenable to have someone in the house at nights. She was not fazed; after all, she had had maids before!

It was explained to her that living standards had changed. No one would be prepared to sleep at the top of the house in cold Spartan conditions with a staircase lit by a single bulb. They might be prepared to accede to her rule that no radio or television should be allowed but more comfortable quarters would have to be provided.

There never was a television at Stonehurst and it was a house rule that the radio was to be kept in the kitchen and only listened to at a time of national emergency. After all, news of any importance could be read in the pages of the Daily Telegraph.

It was agreed that a comfortable room would have to be provided for an attendant. It was concluded that the drawing room, unused for over thirty years, should be spruced up.

The carpet, alas, was found to be crawling with insects. It had been the resting place for many dogs over the years. It was removed by the local authority pest control service.

The chimney was swept, the walls were emulsioned, a new carpet was laid and the room smartened up. Even Lettie, who had little experience of change, was pleased with the result as new life was breathed into the old house. Table surfaces which had not seen daylight for years were revealed. Even the bust of Napoleon appeared to shine.

Lettie was not feeling well, but her spirit was strong. Her doctor was summoned, and, to my surprise, so was I. Lettie wanted me to witness what she had to say.

Dr X (we will spare his blushes by not naming him – by reputation he was a good and caring doctor) arrived. He advised that he did not know what might be the matter with his patient but that she should go into hospital for tests. Lettie's defiant look was a treat to see, her reply quite specific – 'Dr X. You are a fool. You don't take an old woman of nearly 90 to hospital for tests. You take them in to die. I'm not going and I've asked Mr Hartley to be here to ensure that I die in my own bed here at Stonehurst. Good morning'. Wow!

And so, Lettie's bed was brought downstairs to her sitting room and with the reassurance of someone across the hall in the old drawing room, it was felt that proper care was at hand.

The arrangement worked very well and the team of carers arranged their rota between themselves. Lettie was careful to remember them in her will.

Constant reassurance was required about money. Eventually she was satisfied that even at this increased level of expenditure she had enough money to last her until she was 105, which she thought might be sufficient! In any event she was not fearful of death; it was a matter of curiosity – do angels really sing?

Chapter Fourteen

Matrons' Challenge

Lettie's Will had been the subject of much discussion, but she did not wish to be rushed. However the changes in the household showed that the finalisation of her Will should assume some urgency.

After a great deal of thought and discussion, for she did not wish to leave anyone out who had been of service or kindness to her (the lady who saw that her garden gate was shut at night for instance was to receive £100) a final draft could be prepared. This was posted to her on a Friday night. Fate now intervened.

That very night Lettie had a fall and was taken to hospital in Stockport, where she was operated on for a fractured hip. I received the news from one of the carers on the Saturday and went to Stonehurst.

There was the draft will in a typical solicitors' long brown envelope sticking out through the letterbox for anyone to collect. I retrieved it.

My immediate concern was whether or not this Will, which had been so long in the making, would ever be signed. If Lettie was to die without a Will, then she would die intestate. To find out who might be entitled to her estate would involve checking if there were some pretty obscure relations, of whom I had no knowledge.

There being no parents, brothers or sisters, nephews or nieces or issue of theirs, or grandparents, the estate would devolve upon her uncles and aunts or their respective issue if their parents were already dead.

There had been uncles on her mother's side but both those were dead without issue. Her father had two sisters who had married and one of these had a daughter who had no children and who had died in 1963. This I only discovered later.

On what I knew of the family, there were no entitled relatives in which case the estate would go to The Crown. All of this would have to be checked of course, and in the meantime there would be the difficulty of dealing with an uninhabited house. This would not be what Lettie wanted.

With no Will, there would be no legacy to Cicely Craven, a known relative and a long standing friend, but not eligible to inherit on an intestacy because she was a cousin several times removed. Lettie would be unable to thank, through the means of her will, all those people whom she wished to remember. Cicely Craven did in fact predecease Lettie, dying in July 1985.

I set off for Stockport minded to see if Lettie might be lucid enough to sign the agreed draft will. The fact that it was called a draft was merely because it had yet to be finally approved by Lettie.

Here in hospital I found one very frightened old lady in a ward where the beds were cheek by jowl. It was an environment completely alien to her. She spotted me as soon as I came through the swing doors. A loud penetrating voice rang out –'thank God you've come. You've got to get me out of here'. And then as I approached the bed, 'there are n…rs here. Look, there's one coming now'.

This was very embarrassing and I have to say somewhat unexpected from one who had always shown a great deal of tolerance. It was merely that she was not used to strangers. Lack of political correctness was not going to be conducive to a settled ward! I sought out Matron.

She recognised that she had a problem. This was not going to be an easy patient. Lettie was moved to a side ward! She refused to eat any food as she didn't know where it had come from and had a suspicion that it might be tinned and therefore poisonous.

This was not the time to raise the question of signing the Will. I gained the impression that Lettie would survive, if only to get out of the hospital. The body might be frail but the spirit was certainly not broken.

I promised to speak to the Consultant.

The Alexandra Hospital at Cheadle, a private hospital, had a bed available and was prepared to take Lettie. The Consultant recognized that he had a very unhappy patient on his hands. He counselled that any move, so soon after an operation, might result in Lettie's death.

With that advice, I went to see Lettie on the Monday and told her of the risk. She didn't hesitate for a moment – 'I don't mind if I die on the journey, but I am not dying here'. 'And, I need to get home so I can sign my Will'. She moved to a ground floor room in the Alex the following day. A tussle with one Matron therefore ceased but another one was about to begin!

First of all the television. In contrast to other patients, Lettie did not want the television in her room turned on. Well meaning cleaners and ancillary staff, thinking that Lettie could not manage the controls, turned the television on as soon as they came into her room. Before she could protest, the whirlwind staffer had left. Such is the way of hospitals. The bell was rung as Lettie did not know how to turn the hated television off.

Eventually the staff got the message that here was a lady used to living on her own who was quite content to get all her news from The Daily Telegraph. The newspaper was read assiduously; she could even tell you the football scores! Matron should have been warned.

This spat was as nothing to what was to follow, for the second difficulty involved Paula.

Lettie was concerned for Paula. One of the advantages of the Alex was that each patient had a telephone. Lettie didn't like the telephone but she was anxious to see Paula to check that all was well.

Mrs Norton had kindly agreed to take care of the dog whilst Lettie was in hospital. Lettie telephoned her and it was agreed that Paula should be brought to the Alex. How it was arranged I do not know, but Lettie recounted the ensuing adventure with girlish glee.

Fortunately Paula was only a small dog. Somehow Mrs Norton pushed Paula through the open ground floor window of Lettie's room where she was collected by Lettie.

Matron was large and imposing and somewhat reminiscent of Hattie Jacques. Sometime later, when she entered the room, she was rendered speechless at what she saw on Lettie's bed. When she had recovered herself, Matron took a deep breath and said 'What is that?' Lettie, resenting the definitive article, replied, 'this is Paula'. Matron took another deep breath but recognising the determination of her patient, explained firmly, but kindly, that Paula could not be allowed to stay.

Lettie of course knew she was on weak ground but thought she would 'have a go'. She protested that as she was paying £104 per day and Paula could share her food, she saw no reason why Paula could not stay. This cut little ice with Matron.

Paula went home with Mrs Norton!

Lettie went back to Buxton some few days later, staying at Pine Ridge Nursing Home. As part of her recovery programme, she was required to exercise by walking on an even surface with the help of a carer, stick or frame. This is not a problem if you have a full time carer and a 40 feet long hall. There was therefore no point in staying at Pine Ridge and Lettie was soon home. Recuperation was swift and Lettie was soon able to walk assisted only by a stick.

But the Will was still outstanding!

Chapter Fifteen

The Satterthwaite Bequest

The Will was eventually signed on 28 February 1984. It was a 14 page document. There were specific provisions as to Paula, who was kindly taken on by Mrs Norton. There were ten detailed bequests of chattels, 36 monetary legacies to individuals, including shopkeepers, dog lovers and Lettie's carers, nine legacies to different charities and five legacies to different churches with whom the family had had connection.

Lettie had asked me if I would like a picture or two from the many in the house. I asked to have the aquatint of the tug 'Maud'. There was a cluck of disapproval as my choice suggested I had favoured Maud. When I explained that actually I would have preferred the painting of the tug 'Lettie' but that I knew it was to be bequeathed elsewhere, all was well. That picture went to Mr Williams, a retired vet, who had attended to the Satterthwaite dogs over many years.

The two legacies to Christ Church, Burbage, each on slightly different terms, the legacies to St. Mary's Church, Buxton and Overton Church were understandable but I was never to ascertain why King Sterndale Church, outside Buxton, was left £100. There was no obvious connection unless Lettie and Mary had used to walk there and find a bench to sit on.

There had been long discussions as to how Lettie should deal with the balance of her estate after all the legacies. She had relatives, but none of them was close. Those that she wished to benefit were dealt with by way of legacies. What to do with the remainder?

It came down to what had given her pleasure and how best she could help those causes. So she decided that her residuary estate should be divided into two. One half was to go equally to three different animal charities, the RSPCA, the PDSA and the National Canine Defence League. The other half was to form a separate charity which became known as The Satterthwaite Bequest.

Cicely Craven's daughter, Mary, and I were to sort out the chattels at Stonehurst not specifically bequeathed, in accordance with Lettie's wishes. She recognised that this could be quite a big task and I was therefore given a detailed tour of the house.

Lettie died at Stonehurst on 20 March 1986 and was duly buried at Christ Church, Burbage, joining her mother, brother and two sisters. Her estate was sworn at £275,000, but realised much more when the fields opposite Stonehurst were sold for development.

Clearing a house which had been occupied by one family for 70 years and where nothing had been thrown away was a rather daunting task, as was the security of the property.

Very soon after Lettie's death there was evidence that someone had tried to force an entry. I was very concerned, not so much as to the disappearance of a few contents – the house was in a terrible mess – but as to the potential fire hazard.

Here was a large unoccupied house full of papers and magazines, with a large wide wooden staircase, threadbare carpets and curtains hanging in shreds. It was a tinderbox if a match or cigarette was carelessly discarded. It was time to frighten off any potential intruders.

One of my partners came to the rescue. He knew an 'old scoundrel' who would be happy to kip down in the house for a few nights in the company of his Alsatian dog. The cash payment required was quickly agreed and the gentleman concerned made himself comfortable in the cellar. On the first night nothing happened.

The following night, a moonless night by all accounts, at about midnight, our watchman heard the bolts on the trapdoor to the coal cellar being forced and drawn. He laid his hand on his dog to restrain it. Just as two legs appeared to hang down from the trapdoor he let his dog go. With an expletive, the legs quickly disappeared. There were no further unauthorised visitors. Word of the Alsatian dog seemed to spread!

It was important to clear the house quickly. It was a great help that Lettie had specifically bequeathed her pedigree charts relating to flat coated retrievers and all her dog magazines, other pedigree charts and canine equipment to two individuals. Everyone bequeathed any of the chattels co-operated and it was not long before at least the surfaces were cleared of papers, charts and magazines.

Lettie had left all the books in the house to John Rylands Library in Manchester. They were quick to attend as they did not know what to expect.

They described the books from the dining room as the library of a nineteenth-century gentleman, which perhaps gave an indication of their quality. These were Lettie's father's books. There were several first editions and Rylands explained that these would probably replace their later editions in the permanent collection. They seemed well pleased with what they were acquiring.

They were however more excited by the children's books found in the house.

These were in Mrs Satterthwaite's bedroom and had belonged to her as a child. Their good condition was perhaps appropriate considering her upbringing at Disley Parsonage.

As it is unusual to find mid-nineteenth-century children's books, or any children's books, in such condition, John Rylands were delighted with the bequest.

These books, together with other children's books, now form a collection which is called 'The Satterthwaite Collection' at John Rylands Library. It consists of over 1,000 items comprising children's books from the 1860s to the 1930s. The collection is apparently regularly consulted by designers of children's clothes.

The dining room portraits went off to Wythenshawe Hall, a sixteenth-century property owned by the City of Manchester. No comment was made

The Bandstand, Pavilion Gardens, Buxton (2019)

as to whether or not there was a Hogarth amongst them (ante p. 54)

The bulk of the remaining contents were to go to auction. It was difficult to find a firm who would come at short notice but Phillips and Son of Leeds rose to the challenge, intrigued by the description that nothing in the house had been touched for 70 years. They arrived, for their first visit, with two enormous furniture vans, a large removal staff and a valuer.

At first glance, they may have been disappointed. They were faced with threadbare carpets and curtains, faded armchairs with their stuffing bulging out and what had once been decent furniture but now suffering from exposure to sunlight, lack of polish and water damage from standing plants. However, as they explained, it was all period stuff.

War Memorial, St. Mary's Church, Buxton (2019)

Some dining chairs caused genuine excitement. There were five matching Queen Anne chairs scattered about the house, some covered with papers, two in the kitchen, two without their seats. But where was the sixth?

Phillips explained that a set of six matching Queen Anne chairs, even without their seats, would be a much more valuable lot than a mere five chairs.

After an extensive search, the sixth chair was found in a top floor store room, propping up a table. Alas, in spite of the excitement, the set did not make a lot of money in the auction room.

It took Phillips two days to clear the house of what they considered could be sold.

The local scouts took the remaining items for their own sales. Threadbare towels, rugs and blankets with holes in them, an amazing assortment of kitchen cutlery and crockery, kettles and pans, enamel buckets, cleaning mops, several vacuum cleaners of museum vintage, ancient electric fires – all these could apparently be sold. As the scoutmaster told me –'a penny raised from these is a penny we don't have to raise elsewhere'.

The house itself was sold pretty quickly and was soon divided into two dwellings with capacious rooms.

As mentioned, one half of Lettie's residuary estate established The Satterthwaite Bequest. This was set up as a charitable trust to 'benefit wholly or mainly the inhabitants of the former Borough of Buxton'. The geographical area of benefit is thus limited to the old borough boundaries prior to the reorganisation of local government in 1974.

The Satterthwaite Bequest is registered with the Charity Commissioners (registered no. 519179) and now has an annual income of approximately £7,000 to distribute.

To date the Trustees have supported many local charitable causes – Buxton and District Civic Association, Buxton Cricket, Bowling and Lawn Tennis Club, Burbage Band, various Scout and Guide Packs, several town Football clubs, Buxton Sea Cadets, a number of local churches and Buxton Wells Dressing, to name but a few.

The trustees' intention is to benefit as many young people as possible. Whilst Lettie did not have any children herself she always expressed herself interested in their activities. In a naive sort of way she thought that children were little different from dogs in that they needed training and involvement. And she certainly knew a lot about dogs!

The Trustees have also supported the restoration of Solomon's Temple, the bandstand in the Pavilion Gardens and the War Memorial at St. Mary's Church.

The Trustees do not give grants to individuals as they wish to benefit as many people as possible by giving to organisations, such as those mentioned.

The income is not vast, but it is hoped that by a regular drip feed of income into local activities the community of Buxton can benefit.

Lettie was always grateful to the town of Buxton, where she had lived for 70 years. She appreciated its people and loved its countryside. Whilst not mixing socially with the local people nor taking part in local activities, this did not lessen her respect for 'decent Derbyshire folk'. She observed, and the establishment of The Satterthwaite Bequest in her Will was her way of saying 'thank you'.

Lettie's signature (1984)

Appendix 1:
Map of Sunderland Point

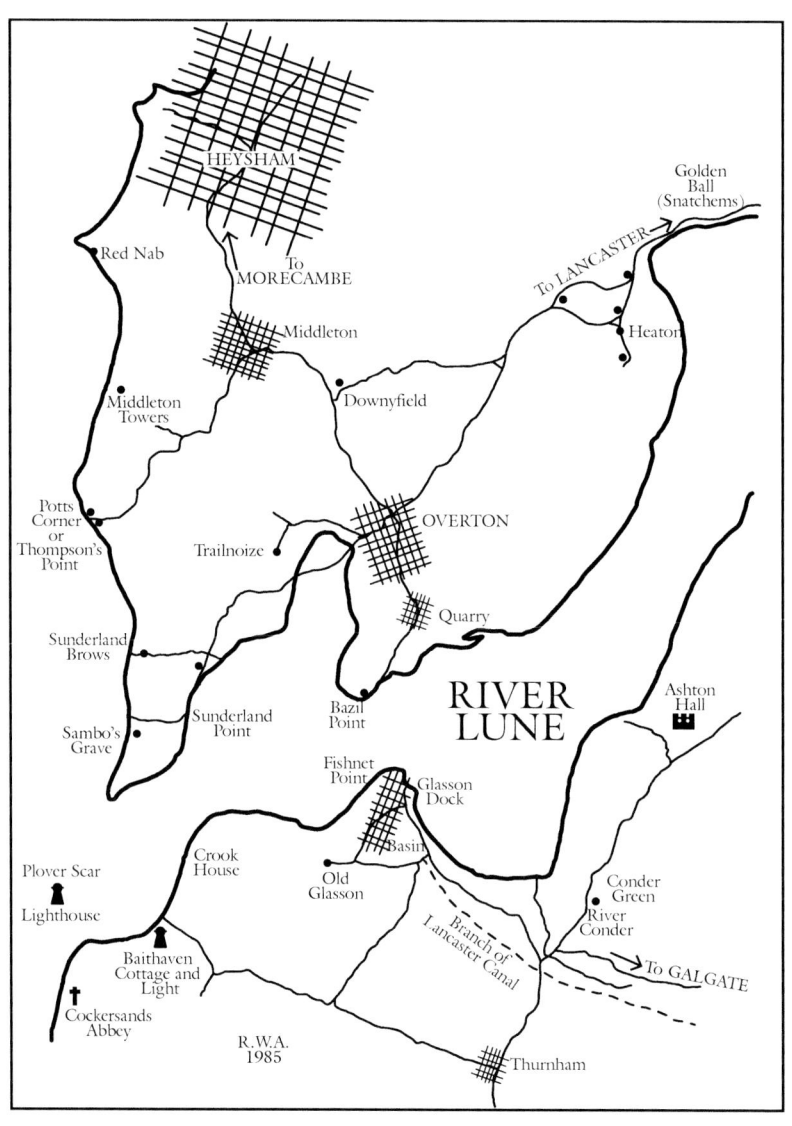

Acknowledgements

It was Mary Mackenzie who persuaded me to put pen to paper before memories of the Buxton Satterthwaites were lost. It is thanks to her that this book has been written.

Mary and Tony Cuffe, Satterthwaite relatives, have been most kind in looking out papers, providing information and lending me the sketch books, photo albums and diaries of Victoria Susan Satterthwaite (nee Hornby). Without their help and encouragement this little histoire could not have been written. I am most grateful to them for their support and enthusiasm.

I was greatly heartened by the willingness of Joanne Wilson of the Samuel Johnson Birthplace Museum in Lichfield to dig out details of Lettie's 1982 visit. This enabled me to connect the Satterthwaites with the Sheridans.

The volunteers at the Family History Society of Cheshire could not have been more helpful and showed their true skills in helping to trace members of the Sheridan family. Their sleuthing was most rewarding.

The Mason-Hornbys of Dalton were kind enough to let me view the 'new' Dalton Hall and its lovely gardens.

Andrew and Carol Johnson of Lancaster 'introduced me' to John Satterthwaite and to the connections with the slave trade of St. Kitts. Their hospitality and help are much appreciated.

Giles Wingate Saul put me in touch with his aunt, Mrs Lawrence, who had visited Stonehurst in the 1960s and provided a graphic description of the hospitality she 'enjoyed'.

David Shore of the Moorside Historical Society provided me with information about Sunderland Point and both he, and Stephen Kelsall, were keen that I should mention Sambo's Grave.

My sister-in-law Val Hartley brought her critical eye to the manuscript and I hope that I have profited from her advices and suggestions.

Margaret Davison, who helped with my book *An Oldham Velvet Dynasty*, has once again brought her skill and expertise as a photographer to enhance this book. Her photographs of the side view of Stonehurst, Disley Chruch, the present day Dalton Hall, Overton Church and the Satterthwaite Grave at Burbage have brought the descriptions in the book alive. She also introduced me to Sally Phipps-Hornby who provided further confirmation of the connections between the Hornby and Satterthwaite families.

Dr John Tomlinson, a native of Lancaster, lent me his much prized booklet relating to the Letterbook of Benjamin Satterthwaite. This provided valuable insight relating to the early family. His interest has been greatly appreciated.

Luisa O'Hara used her computer skills to my advantage, putting all the illustrations in their proper order.

To all of the above, and to others who have offered help, advice and assistance, I express my grateful thanks.

I hope that I have acknowledged all appropriate sources, but if I have erred a communication to the publishers should be made so that future acknowledgements are given.

Select Bibliography

Books

Bolton King, R., *Buxton College 1675–1970* (privately published, 1973)
Cunliffe, Hugh, *The Story of Sunderland Point* (Hugh Cunliffe and Trelawny Press Limited: Morecambe, 1985 and R. W. Atkinson, 2008)
Dickens, Charles, *Bleak House* (1853; Penguin Classics: London, 1971)
Egerton, Mrs Fred, *Admiral of the Fleet Sir Geoffrey Phipps Hornby* (William Blackwood & Sons: Edinburgh and London, 1896)
Flanders, Judith, *A Circle of Sisters* (Penguin Books: London, 2002)
Hall, Radclyffe, *The Unlit Lamp* (Virago Modern Classics: London, 1981)
Hurd, Douglas, and Edward Young, *Disraeli* (Weidenfeld and Nicolson: London, 2013)
Sadler, Nigel, *The Slave Trade* (Shire Library: London, 2009)
Schofield, M. M., *The Letter Book of Benjamin Satterthwaite* (Lancaster Library: Lancaster, 1960)
Thomas, Hugh *The Slave Trade: The Story of the Atlantic Slave Trade 1440–1870* (Simon and Schuster: New York, 1999)
Welvin, James, *A Short History of Slavery* (Penguin Books: London, 2007)
Woodward, E. L., *The Age of Reform 1815–1870* (Oxford University Press: Oxford, 1938)

Journals, articles and guides

Burns, Karen, 'Fanny's Hand' (Castle Park Stories: Lancaster, 2013)
'Guidebook to Leighton Hall' (Jarrold Publishing: Peterborough, 2008)
'Knowsley Hall' (The Stanley Estate and Stud Company and Jarrold Publishing: Peterborough, 2003)
Siberling, Norman J., 'British Financial Experience 1790–1830', in *The Review of Economics and Statistics*, volume 1 (JSTOR, 1919)

Index

T̲ʜᴇ ɴᴀᴍᴇs ᴏғ ғᴇᴍᴀʟᴇs who married are listed under their maiden name, with a cross reference to their married name where page details are given. Names of places or persons who are unlikely to occur to be mentioned more than once may not have been indexed.

Alexandra Hospital, Cheadle 97

Bazil 37, 41, 75
Bolten, Letitia Christiana (see Sheridan)
Broad Chalke, near Salisbury 70, 71
Buxton, Derbyshire 1, 3, 66, 69

Casson, Jane (1719–1803) 42
Chantry, Disley and Winwick 30
Christ Church, Burbage, Buxton 81, 89, 99, 100
Craven, Mrs Cicely Mary (nee Townley) (1907–85) 78, 81, 89, 90, 97
Cross Hill, Torrisholme, nr Morecambe 75

Dalton Hall, Burton in Westmorland 14, 15, 20, 21, 23, 75
Derby, 12th Earl of (1752–1834) 16
Derby, 13th Earl of (1775–1851) 16, 19
Derby, 14th Earl of (1799–1869) 17, 18, 29
Derbyshire County Council 94
Disley, Cheshire 3, 14, 15, 25

Eton College 33, 64, 65

Fanny's Hand (Frances Elizabeth Johnson) 44

Gillow, Richard (1772–1849) 46
Gillow, Richard (1733–1811) 45, 46
Gillow, Robert (1704–72) 37, 40, 45
Gillow, Robert (1745–93) 45
Glasson Dock, Lancaster 37, 38, 42
Gore-Jones, Agnes (nee Spankie) (d.1912) 54
Gore-Jones, Arabella Louisa (see Satterthwaite)
Gore-Jones, John (1796–1879) 54
Gore-Jones, Letitia Elizabeth (nee Sheridan) (d.1852) 54, 55
Gore-Jones, William Brydges Neynoe (1826–88) 54, 55
Grange, The, Kenley 1, 60

Hogarth, William (1697–1764) 54, 102
Hopwood, Rev. J. (d.1890) 29
Hornby, Charlotte Margaret (see Stanley)
Hornby, Charlotte Smith (nee Stanley) (d.1805) 16
Hornby, Edmund (1773–1857) 16, 18
Hornby, Edmund George (Mundo) (1799–1865) 19, 28
Hornby, Edmund Geoffrey Stanley (1839–1923) 21
Hornby, Brig Gen. Edmund John Phipps (1857–1947) 33

INDEX

Hornby, Col. Geoffrey Hardinge Phipps (1889–1967) 33
Hornby, Capt. Geoffrey Stanley Phipps (1856–1927) 33
Hornby, Rev. Geoffrey (1750–1812) 16, 29, 31
Hornby, Rev. James John (1777–1855) 29
Hornby, John James (Provost of Eton) (1826–1909) 33, 64
Hornby, Lucy Smith (nee Stanley) (d.1833) 16, 29
Hornby, Admiral Sir Phipps (1785–1867) 31
Hornby, Admiral Sir Geoffrey Thomas Phipps (1825–95) 30, 32
Hornby, Admiral Robert Stewart Phipps (1866–1956) 33
Hornby, Sarah (nee Yates) 19
Hornby, Victoria Susan (see Satterthwaite)

Johnson Birthplace Museum, Lichfield 52, 92
Johnson Dictionary 52, 53
Johnson, Mrs Pamela 82
Johnson, Dr Samuel (1709–84) 91, 92
Jones – see Gore Jones

Knowsley Hall, Merseyside 17, 20

Lancaster, City of 36, 40
Langford, Miss Janet May (1894–1984) 66
Lawrence, Mrs Diana 82, 89
Legh of Lyme Hall 28, 30
Legh, Piers 30
Leighton Hall, Carnforth 46
Lichfield, Johnson Birthplace Museum 52, 92
Lune, River 37, 38
Lyme Hall, Cheshire 30, 31
Lyons, Col. Charles (1690–1780) 53

Mason-Hornby, Anthony Fielden (1931–94) 22
Mason-Hornby, Francis Anthony (1961–) 105
Michaelson, Millicent (nee Satterthwaite) 51

Norton, Mrs Sandra 94, 98, 99

Overton, Morecambe 36, 38, 41, 75, 99

Paula (Lettie's dog) 98
Pennant, Adelaide Wynne (see Satterthwaite)
Penrhyn-Hornby, Charles Windham Leycester (1873–1966) 22, 76
Pickford and Co. 55 ,56
Postlethwaite, Elizabeth (nee Satterthwaite) 51

Quakers 42, 47, 48

Ram's Head, Disley 74
Rawlins, Mary Stedman (see Satterthwaite)
Rawlins, Stedman (d. 1788) 39, 41
Romney, George (Artist) 40
Ruddy, Aileen Beatrice Clifford (d. 1951) 76, 78
Rylands Library, John. Manchester 100, 101

Sambo's Grave 42, 43
Satterthwaite, Adelaide Wynne (nee Pennant) (1871–1960) 70, 72
Satterthwaite, Arabella Louisa (nee Gore-Jones) (c.1830–1902) 55, 56
Satterthwaite, Beatrice Mary (Mary) (1899–1976) 9, 11, 13, 60, 67, 68, 69, 79
Satterthwaite, Benjamin (1718–92) 40, 42, 45, 47
Satterthwaite Bequest 99, 103
Satterthwaite, Charles (1786–1815) 51
Satterthwaite, Charles Geoffrey (1873–1935) 3, 61, 70, 72–78
Satterthwaite, Rev Charles James (1834–1910) 15, 25, 27, 30, 33, 34, 35, 38, 42, 74
Satterthwaite, Charles Sheridan (1811–97) 48, 51, 52, 53, 55, 56
Satterthwaite Collection at John Rylands Library 101
Satterthwaite, Rev.Edmund James (1866–1922) 70, 72, 74
Satterthwaite, Elizabeth (see Postlethwaite)

Satterthwaite, Evelyn Letitia (Lettie) (1895–1986) 8, 25, 60, 62, 67, 68, 69, 79, 85, 87, 90–100, 103
Satterthwaite, Frances Nanette (Anna) Georgiana (nee Sheridan) (1790–1816) 51, 53, 54, 55, 91
Satterthwaite, Francis Edmund Sheridan (Frank) (1892–1955) 60, 63, 64–66, 79, 80
Satterthwaite, Francis Neynoe (1815–1838) 51
Satterthwaite, Gertrude Mary Charlotte (1861–1954) 14, 42, 62, 79, 80, 81
Satterthwaite, James Cornelius (1798–1857) 15, 35, 38, 41, 48, 51
Satterthwaite, John (1743–1807) 39, 40, 41, 44, 45, 47–51, 54
Satterthwaite, John Arthur Sheridan (1857–1915) 1, 14, 42, 48, 56
Satterthwaite, Mary (Polly) Stedman (d.1837) 39, 48, 49, 55
Satterthwaite, Maud Gertrude (1891–1982) 10, 12, 25, 57, 60, 63, 67, 81–90
Satterthwaite, Millicent (1791–?) (see Michaelson)
Satterthwaite, Thomas (1684–1728) 47
Satterthwaite, Victoria Susan (nee Hornby) (1837–1906) 15, 19, 25, 26, 28, 38, 42, 60
Sheridan, Charles Francis (1750–1806) 52, 53
Sheridan, Letitia Christiana (nee Bolten) (d. 1813) 53
Sheridan, Frances Nanette (Anna) Georgiana (see Satterthwaite)
Sheridan, Letitia Elizabeth (see Gore-Jones)
Sheridan, Richard Brinsley (1751–1816) 52
Sheridan, Thomas (1719–88) 52, 91
Slave Trade Act 1807 41
Solomon's Temple, Buxton 47, 63, 68, 103
Spankie, Agnes (see Gore-Jones)
St. Kitts, West Indies 39, 40
St. Mary's Church, Buxton 87, 88, 89, 99, 103
Stanley, Charlotte Margaret (nee Hornby) (d.1817) 16
Stanley, Lady Charlotte Smith (see Hornby)
Stanley, Lady Lucy Smith (see Hornby)
Stockport Infirmary 96
Stonehurst, Green Lane, Buxton 4, 5, 60, 79, 91, 94
Sunderland Point, Lancaster 37, 42

Thames Steam Tug and Lighterage Co. Limited 2, 56, 57, 64
Townley, Cicely Mary (see Craven)
Tufnell Satterthwaite & Co. Limited 2, 4, 64

Waller, Miss 19, 28
Waring and Gillow 45, 46
Williams-Ellis, Sir Bertram Clough (Architect) (1883–1978) 22
Wilson, Rev. Noble (d. 1859) 26, 34
Wingate Saul, Sir Ernest KC 82
Winwick Church, St. Oswalds 29, 30
Wythenshawe Hall, Manchester 101